Dying To Live

Death and The Afterlife

By

Colette Brown

Copyright 2020 © Colette Brown

All rights reserved. No part of this publication may be reproduced or distributed in any form or by any means, electronic or mechanical, including photocopying, recording, or by any information storage or retrieval system, without the prior written consent of the author.

ISBN: 9798670929523

For Alexander

"The ones that love us never really leave us."
- Sirius Black (Harry Potter)

Table of Contents

Introduction 1

Start a Conversation 5

Taboos and Dead Bodies 9

Premonitions of Death 16

Near-Death Experiences 20

The Soul Leaves the Body 28

The Spirits Gather 31

The Afterlife 41

Miscarriage, Termination, and IVF 49

When A Child Dies 58

Suicide 68

When An Animal or Pet Dies 78

Animal Messages From Over The Rainbow Bridge 84

Bereavement and Navigating Grief 97

Messages From The Spirit World 111

How To Prepare for a Good Death 131

Acknowledgments	137
References	140
Resources	141

Introduction

This wasn't the book that I had decided to write. I felt that I deserved a break from the intense, emotional prose of my last book, Memoirs of a Clairvoyant. That book had been draining and very cleansing but had left me without words for a few months. Normally I would write some fiction or short stories after a difficult book simply to restore my balance and energy. To this effect, I had started to write a paranormal thriller with spirits and karma and delightful twists of fate. Yet, it never felt right. The characters never filled out to the stage where I could remember their life details, even their hair colour changed from paragraph to paragraph. Those who have read my novels know that I normally feel a 'realness' about my characters which eventually wrecks me when I have to say goodbye to them. So, this paranormal thriller felt like it was being written by someone else and I was only some sort of voyeur. It was the right book but at the wrong time. But I persevered because I am a Taurus with the capacity for stubbornness unrivalled by other astrological signs.

Then on a day where I had given myself a break from writing, four separate messages changed my mind and the contract with the Universe to write this book was agreed. The first message was on social media from a woman who nursed end of life patients. She asked me if I would ever think about writing a book about death and the afterlife, as she felt it would be a wonderful resource for her to help with discussions with patients and their families. I was taken aback as I had never really thought of writing a mediumship book. However, I said I would think about it and thanked her for the suggestion. The second push came from yet another person who helped counsel people regarding terminal illness. She felt that there were a lot of resources available on the psychological aspect of dying but that she was frequently stumped when asked about an afterlife and what it may be like, especially by someone who did not have a religion to guide them. She had enjoyed my mediumship videos on YouTube and felt that I had helped her with my insights. These two requests came within hours of one another.

My brain was whirling, wondering if I could use my experience of seeing and hearing spirits and glimpsing the afterlife as an accessible book for those who needed it. When this excitement comes over me, I know that I have found what I should be writing about. This hadn't happened with my paranormal thriller book which I had put work into and wasn't yet ready to cast aside to start from scratch on a new idea. The idea of moving on and doing all the groundwork again was just too much to contemplate. It was a year since my memoirs and although it was still selling, it wasn't in quantities that could be described as an income. I needed a book out within months simply for financial reasons. I decided to continue with my thriller and write the afterlife book after that had been published.

Then an old acquaintance hailed me on Facebook. I had known her for many years due to clairvoyant readings and events. She told me that she had cancer and it was terminal and that she didn't have very long left to live. I was horrified and sad. She asked me if I could do something for her. I said of course and she asked me if I could just reassure her about the afterlife. She believed in it but felt the need to hear my experiences as she had in the past. I gladly chatted with her and then said a sad goodbye. She died three weeks later.

My mind was full of sadness for this woman and her family that night as I went through some messages that had been sent to me. One was from a man that I didn't know but it contained a poem about...death and the afterlife. It was a deep poem, but it wasn't the poem itself that made me shiver. It was its subject matter. For the fourth time in one day I had been prodded to think about the afterlife. I knew then that I would put aside my paranormal thriller and start writing what the Universe seemed to be instructing me to write. I knew I wanted to help people understand the spiritual aspect of death and know the contentment of believing in an afterlife if that is what they should choose. The problem seemed to me that death is still very much a taboo subject in the western 'modern' society in which I live.

"When a person is born, we rejoice, and when they're married we are jubilant, but when they die we try to pretend nothing has happened."
Margaret Mead

"What's wrong with death sir? What are we so mortally afraid of? Why can't we treat death with a certain amount of humanity and dignity, and decency, and God forbid, maybe even humour. Death is not the enemy gentlemen. If we're going to fight a disease, let's fight one of the most terrible diseases of all, indifference."
Patch Adams

I felt I had a lot to say because of my life and my career as a clairvoyant medium but I knew the book would be better if it had many voices. So, I started the long process of collating peoples' stories of the death of loved ones and also the proof they had that they lived on. There was nothing scientific about this, although I have a scientific background. All the stories are anecdotal. I present them for you simply because they resonate with what I have experienced in my day to day life and also my professional life before I retired. I remember a story about a student who asked an old Native American elder to explain what the Great Mystery was in his spiritual path. The elder replied, "Well, it wouldn't be a great mystery if we knew what the Great Mystery was, would it?" I feel this applies to our view of the afterlife. I feel that our brains couldn't cope with the full knowledge of the next level of our existence, so glimpses are all we are meant to have, for now. Maybe after many more years of evolution we will be more attuned to the vibration of our next level but for now, all we have are glimpses by ourselves, mediums, and shamans. For the full experience, we have to die to live it.

I hope you enjoy my book. I hope you will think about the stories and be open to some of the signs folk received from spirit. I hope the descriptions of dying and passing over will show that you need not fear it. I thank everyone who trusted me with their precious stories, safe in the knowledge that you will have helped many people. Finally, I hope this book starts conversations about death and what lies beyond. Death should not be taboo. We all must do it! We are all dying from the moment we are born. The only difference is the length of our journeys.

Start a Conversation

"The first breath is the beginning of death."
- Thomas Fuller

We do need to talk. Seriously, we need to talk. We need to talk and ask questions and tell stories about, become familiar with, tolerant of and not fear...death. We live in a time when there has never been greater access to information. If we don't understand something or need information on how to do something we can Google it, watch a video on YouTube, read a Reddit, or ask for an opinion on our Twitter feeds. We can ask a Facebook friend, look at a photo on Instagram, or, for a quick answer, go on Snapchat. We can find information on anything. There is almost too much information out there, but it isn't personal to us. Sadly, we only seem to talk about death as it affects us; when it threatens to descend on us or our loved ones. We talk about it when it becomes intensely personal and by then it might be too late to understand the process and the needs of the individual - whether that be the dying person or the one that loves them. We suffer from stiff upper lip syndrome and subconsciously feel that if we don't address the elephant in the room that it perhaps might not trample all over us...for a time anyway.

Death is a hard conversation. It is a recognition of our fragility and our smallness. It forces us to face up to the thought that one day, we simply won't be here. We won't exist in this human plane of existence. That we aren't immortal in the sense of living here forever. Yet the conversation about death is one we need to have with ourselves, our loved ones, and our society. If you follow a spiritual path it is a conversation you need to have with your deity, your ancestors, your higher self, or the cosmos. There needs to be conversations of what you might expect, what you might feel and what you might experience because without these conversations there can only be fear. If something is unknown, we can fear it. When something is more familiar, we can learn to accept it and therefore lose our fear. This is important for us individually but also as a species because a species living in fear of dying can make some stupid choices. Life becomes so precious a commodity that it is clung on to by any means. Life becomes either a time of glorified materialism or a time of religious cultism. Any outlet can be chosen so that our primal fear of 'not being' can be at least blunted whether that be by drugs, alcohol, narcissism, or celebrity worship. Instead of seeing death as a rebirth or new beginning, it is seen as the end. The closer we come to the end of something we crave, the more we hold on without dignity and an open mind.

> *"Preparing for death is one of the most empowering things you can do. Thinking about death clarifies your life."*
> Candy Chang

In times gone by, death was dealt with normally at home, surrounded by family, and was a natural progression of life. It was sad, heart-breaking, and so very normal. There was support, there was someone to talk to and cry on. There were stories of spirits and deities and even some humour at times. There were rituals. There was hope. If we saw that someone we knew had survived after the loss of a loved one, we felt that we could too. The family or community looked after its own and it learned and developed strength from its losses. In societies that are more tribal or where generations of families live together, we see less fear of death and more of an acceptance of the seasons of life. But now people can live in their thousands in one skyscraper yet never connect with their next-door neighbours. Our support system has gone and we are not comfortable discussing taboo subjects unless they are on reality TV and make for good ratings. And so, we all suffer.

We suffer because we push the idea of death away. This not only affects our ability to talk to loved ones about their wants and needs for their passing but also stunts our progress in finding our own good death. And all the time there is the background noise and never-ending trivia that takes the place of plain conversation about the end of life. Talking about death, whether that be our own, or that of a loved one takes courage and a lack of embarrassment. I hope once you have read this book that you find what you need to have probably the most important conversation you will ever have: What death means for you. I aim to share my own experiences of the death process from a spiritual perspective, as an individual, and from my work as a medium. I will also be sharing the stories of those who watched their loved one's pass, those who had near-death experiences, and those who received proof of the afterlife from those who journeyed before them. I hope to help you transcend the fear of not existing or of not being you anymore. I hope to help you understand the spiritual death process so that you can help your family members and friends as they undergo their personal death experience. I hope to open your mind to the potential that the afterlife is real and that the energy that is us simply doesn't disappear. I hope through peoples' stories to show you that the soul, the consciousness that we know and love as mother, father, child, spouse, sibling, or pet lives on in another place that is very close to where we are right now.

> *"It's only when we truly know and understand that we have a limited time on earth – and that we have no way of knowing when our time is up – that we will begin to live each day to the fullest as if it was the only one we had."*
> Elisabeth Kubler-Ross

Taboos and Dead Bodies

Dylan Thomas wrote the words below.

> *"Do not go gentle into that good night*
> *Old age should burn and rave at close of day*
> *Rage, rage against the dying of the light."*

Why would I disagree with Dylan Thomas? The answer is - because he is wrong. We should not rave, burn, or rage as we die. We should look into the light and go gently with dignity and honour towards the new life that awaits us. We should not fear what lies beyond the veil. Neither should we try to hang on to a life that has reached its conclusion. We all die. No-one has a 'get out of jail free' card with death. From the moment our souls arrive in our bodies, we are already on the path to death. Life is amazing. It is worth the trauma of birth. Our afterlife is amazing. It is worth the trauma of death. How do I know? I have glimpsed it and had spirits come back to tell me about it. I do not need faith to believe in the afterlife. I know in my heart and my mind that it exists. Even science shows that energy can change form and simply doesn't stop being energy. The You that is You doesn't disappear when you die. It simply leaves its human container and moves on to another realm.

Yet we fear death and avoid talking about it as though somehow talking about it might make it happen. We don't talk about our deaths to our children and loved ones. We don't voice our fears or our hopes in case we upset them or disturb the status quo. When a family member is dying, we don't find out what they want or need. We don't encourage them to communicate. Sometimes we tell them they are going to be fine when they clearly will not get better. Why the lies? Modern western societies have lost the understanding of death as a process. In other countries and in more tribal or less 'civilised' societies we see a healthy understanding of death as a part of life and the need for a good death. By a 'good' death I mean that the particular death may have been prepared for, talked about and the ritual or ceremony planned years previously. The dying person and their family would be given space and time to be part of the passing. Many religions and cultures have retained the knowledge of how to die well.

*"As a well-spent day brings happy sleep,
so life well used brings happy death."*
Leonardo DaVinci

I have Hindu friends whose father travelled back to India to partake in his death rites years ago after his wife passed. He is still alive but is an example of someone who is contented, has no fear, and in his heart is prepared for his turn. In doing these rites he also allowed his children to know that he wanted to be ready when his time came and also expressed his requests for his funeral and sorted his practical concerns. His family will be devastated when he passes but he has made it easier for them by showing that he is not afraid of death and understands that he is going to a good place because he has lived a good life.

Now look at how we handle death in our so-called modern and more 'civilised' societies: we don't talk about death as a natural part of living. We go silent when someone mentions death, and this shuts them up for fear of offending our sensibilities. In doing this we have deprived the person and ourselves of deep understanding of hope and fears. We may mention in passing where insurance policies are kept and maybe what song we would like played at our funeral but in seeing potential hurt and sadness in our loved one's eyes, we move on to talk about the weather and something is lost in that moment. We lose our chance to understand both points of view. We lose the chance to educate or pass on old stories and death once again retreats into the shadows of our minds only to push forth separately in the night-time hours when we can't communicate and must lie with words unsaid. Communication is necessary if all are to see death as something that could be approached in a way in which everyone gains.

Look at the way in which we treat dead bodies. I worked as an auxiliary nurse in a geriatric unit during my university holidays. When someone died the nurses did a wonderful job of washing and preparing the body for relatives to see. This was done with respect and love and I will forever be grateful to have observed this. Yet, when the body had to be transported out of the ward, all the individual room doors were closed. Then a big steel box on wheels came creaking and clanking along the corridor, the body was placed inside, wheeled away and the doors were opened again. Then the life of the ward went on with excess cheer to compensate for the 'time out' that the death had caused. Even at age seventeen, I questioned why all the doors were closed when truly everyone knew what was happening. I was told it was to respect the living who were near death themselves. Maybe seeing the box would in some way remind them that they too would be in it soon? I felt that this attitude of honouring the living dishonoured the person who had died. The false sense of cheer afterward also negated the solemnity that could have been used to open conversations and reassure those nearing or fearing, death. By then I had already had a life of seeing spirits and knew that the afterlife was simply a step away. I was more on the side of the person whose body was being secreted out of the ward as though they were guilty of something horrible...the final crime...they died!

That was over forty years ago, and I have seen things change for the better. Now, in nursing homes, the dead person is covered and transported through the front door while those who wish to can line the hall and honour the person, say a prayer, and let grief out. I have also seen videos of the walk of honour in hospitals for a person who has donated their organs so that others may benefit. Nurses, doctors, and members of the public line the corridors and clap or sing as the body is taken to the morgue. The respect in the air is tangible and something to see. It is life-affirming.

My daughter was at her granda's side when he died and says one of the things that made her heart soar was the respect shown to his body by the undertakers. She watched from the window as they gently put his body in the back of the hearse, closed the door and they both stood back and bowed to the body before taking it on its journey. This respect for her granda's body meant the world to her.

"I have seen death too often to believe in death,
It is not an ending, but a withdrawal.
As one who finishes a long journey.
Stills the motor. Turns off the lights
Steps from the car
And walks up the path
To the home that awaits him"
Unknown

In western culture we rarely see dead bodies. We see death in so many tv shows, films, and games yet these false deaths, these unreal dead bodies do not represent the truth in any way. In times past, and still in more tribal societies, people died at home. Families knew how to prepare the body for the funeral or burial. They knew how to honour the body of the person they had loved. Various forms of ritual were handed down from generation to generation and most people would have seen a dead body before they hit maturity. Now many people die in hospitals or nursing homes. This means that the age that people see their first dead body can be into their twenties or thirties and even then, it will have been prepared and sanitised and may not resemble the person in life.

I remember seeing my first dead body when I was sixteen. My beloved gran had passed. She had had a stroke in the hospital so when I first saw her after she died it was in the funeral parlour. Many things shocked me about her dead body. Yet I'm glad I viewed it. It convinced me that she as a person - her essence, her soul - was no longer associated with the cold, hard body. My wonderful vibrant Gran who in life was warm, gentle, silly, and cuddly was now a cold shell that bore no relation to the woman I loved. Her features were strange. Her colour was wrong. Her eyes were closed, and her mouth glued into a thin, straight line. The worst thing was the coldness of her body. No one had told me that a dead body could be so cold. Her fingers were held in prayer and felt like some form of set clay. I pulled away and sat in the corner. Through my tears, I had a distinct recognition that my dear gran's body was just the husk of her. I knew she simply wasn't there anymore. Her soul had left its earthly chariot. I still loved her body and would honour it simply because it had hosted her soul. It was the physical way I had connected to her, but it wasn't her. I knew I had always connected with her soul, her personality. Where now was her loving nature? Where now what's her gentle laugh? Where now was her intellect, her joy, her love? They weren't here anymore. They didn't reside in this used up body. They had flown with her soul back to Source. I will never regret seeing my gran in her coffin because even though her spirit had flown, I could honour her body and say goodbye to it. It was cathartic and freeing.

When my dad died, he was in a nursing home and the first time I saw his body was at the funeral parlour after it had been worked on. This time I was distressed but could see great humour in the way he looked and I am sure my dad would have been laughing too. In life, he had quite bushy eyebrows that needed to be trimmed and tamed every week. He used to joke that if he left them to grow, he would look like Groucho Marx. The undertaker had applied a harsh black colour to my dad's silver eyebrows, and he looked like a comic book villain. After the initial shock, I couldn't stop laughing. It was bizarre. Once again came the knowledge that this dead body was just a husk. I kissed his forehead and left the room. My dad's soul was already on its journey. On both occasions seeing my gran and my dads' dead bodies had given me closure. I will never regret seeing them.

Yet sometimes it may not be appropriate to see the dead body. If the body has been deteriorating or has been disfigured in some way, then this can be harder than not seeing the body. My mum in law died abroad and it took time for her body to be flown home. At this point, the professional funeral director advised against seeing the body. This was the correct decision, but I do know that some of her grandchildren did not have the closure they needed. In this situation, I believe it was about choosing the lesser of two evils.

My mum died in her home during the night. She lived in sheltered housing and had buzzed the carer when she felt ill. I was called by the police as the first contact. When I arrived, she had been placed in bed and covers pulled up. She looked asleep. Her body was still warm and touching her and kissing her and holding her hand felt very special. When my sister arrived, we combed her hair and made sure she was in her favourite nightie. We lit scented candles and sat with her until the doctor came to pronounce her dead. This doctor had known her for many years and was visibly upset. It felt special that he had made the call. As he left, my mum's priest arrived to do the ceremony of last rites. My mum and dad had been married in his parish church when it had first opened. There was a bit of embarrassment on my behalf as I had forgotten the prayers as I had walked away from organised religion after my dad had died. It was a beautiful ceremony. The bedroom felt sacred and special and it felt like my mum was still there although not in her body. My sister and I stayed with my mum's body until the funeral director came to take her to the parlour. My mum's death seemed easier to accept due to the circumstances. She was at home; she was surrounded by her things and she simply looked like she had slept away. There was a joy in being around her and looking after her body that will stay with me. Her passing was more like times of old where a family would look after the dead. I felt far more closure in my mum's passing than my dad and gran's. We were very lucky to have this time with her.

Don't get me wrong, I don't believe that death is easy for those left behind. Losing someone we love is the hardest thing. We will handle it in different ways. There is no correct way to handle the passing of someone we have connected to. Only your way. But the way death is handled by all involved including professionals can mean the difference between surviving the death of the one you love or not being able to come to terms with it. It can mean the difference between grieving for decades rather than years. If we can see that the person was ready to go, that the passing was as it was meant to be, and the formalities have been made easier, then the standard phases of grief can be manifested and understood.

Premonitions of Death

Some people do have premonitions of a loved one's death and this can partially prepare them for the time ahead, should they choose to believe it. I chose not to believe when I had insight into my dad's death. It came in a very odd way. My elder brother had asked for a tarot reading about his life and as I laid the cards out, I saw a combination that, to me, can mean death. It was specifically linked to his relationship with our dad. The timing of the death looked like three months ahead. My mum was about to undergo a knee replacement operation and my dad was due to be in a nursing home for respite care until she was well enough to look after him again. We were more focused on our mum than dad at that time, but I remember feeling a shiver go down my spine and realising that what I had seen for my brother accidentally, would affect me too. I also 'saw' a vision of my dad with one of his eyes looking strange- one of his pupils was massive compared to the other one.

I tried to put it to the back of my mind as I was not in the place to accept it. I had prayed every day that my dad would not suffer after a bad series of strokes and a terrible quality of life and that his spirit family would ease his suffering and take him home. Yet, nine years on, he was still here and the sense that soon he might not be was too much for me to take in.

The night before he died I visited him in the nursing home. He was agitated and wanted to communicate something important to me. He had been left with no language and only certain noises after the strokes. Yet he told me, in his way, that I had to look after my mum and tell her he loved her. I knew what he was saying, even if his sounds made no sense. I am crying reliving this moment. It is hard to write it down. As I looked deeply into his eyes, I noticed that one of his pupils was massive. I felt a cold chill but still would not accept that he may be leaving us.

I went home and saw my daughters and tidied the house and had a restless sleep. The next day after feeding my younger daughter her breakfast and settling her with a bottle of milk, I phoned the nursing home. The secretary said she would get a nurse to talk to me. I felt my heart would burst out of my body. The kind nurse told me that my dad had his breakfast that morning and was sitting in the residents' lounge watching television. A nurse asked him if he wanted some tea and he indicated yes. When she brought his cup over, he was dead. No pain, no drama - he just slipped away as his favourite wee nurse brought him his cup of tea. It was three months to the day since I had given my brother his tarot reading.

My mum lived another two years after my dad passed but was lost without him. One afternoon when I visited, she asked if I could put my eight-year-old daughter, Jennifer, on the phone when I got home so she could talk to her. My younger daughter Jillian was with me and had so many cuddles from her nana. As we prepared to leave, my mum caught both of my hands in hers and said, "I love you so much, do you know that?" I said I did and that I loved her so much too. When I arrived home, I listened in as Jennifer chatted to her nana for quite a while. She finished the call with, "I love you too Nana...so much." It felt so very lovely and heart-warming. I remember going to bed feeling so loved and cherished. The police came to my door at 4am to say that my mum had died and could I go down to be with her. All I could think of was, "She knew! She knew!" This time, I did not know in advance.

I have a friend who is also called Colette Brown. She lives in Canada and has contributed so much to this book. Here is her cousin's premonition dream -

"Cousin Jessie shared a dream that Jim's Mom Margaret (who had passed twelve years before Jim himself did) was coming to greet him with a suitcase and was getting ready to hug him, saying it would be the best Mother's Day ever - this year 2014. I was in shock. I remember talking to God and saying please if it is truly Jim's time come and get him before or after Mother's Day because I did not want such a sad memory on my day. The Lord did hear me because Jim passed on May 8th...a few days before Mother's Day."

Colette Brown Ontario, Canada.

Some people have premonitions of their deaths like Shona's Mum-

"In 1984 my mother told me she was having some 'visitors' at night and when I asked her about it she said it was spirits and she was frightened as she felt something was going to happen. Unfortunately, she took no action and she died of a cardiac arrest a few days later. I always feel she was being given a warning."

Some people can 'feel' when a person has passed or can be visited by the person as they go. As Britney shares with us -

"My father passed away five years ago. We were not close, and he wasn't very present when I was younger, but we began to know each other when I was a late teen. I was new in my relationship with the man who would be my husband (Jim) and I woke up in the middle of the night and saw a man with the silhouette of a cowboy hat standing near the windows of the bedroom. I talked to him thinking it was Jim and said, "What are you doing over there? You're freaking me out," and Jim lying next to me woke up and said, "Who are you talking to?" I glanced at Jim and by the time I realised it was not him and looked back the man was gone. Well, a week later I got the call that my father had died the week prior. He had a big tattoo on his arm of a skull with a cowboy hat on. I knew immediately that was my father saying goodbye."

Britney Lynne Merrigan-Nelson

Near-Death Experiences

"End? No, the journey doesn't end here. Death is just another path...one that we all must take. The gray rain-curtain of this world rolls back, and all turns to silver glass... And then you see it. White shores... and beyond, a far green country under a swift sunrise."
J.R.R. Tolkien

Near-Death Experiences or NDEs have been reported in literature, philosophy, and science for thousands of years. They are surprisingly common. In 1982 a Gallop poll showed that over five percent of the population of the USA had reported having one. We have many anecdotal accounts. Just key in Near-Death Experiences on YouTube or Google and prepare to be shocked. NDE is a phenomenon that we think we know a bit about but that very few people can express knowledge of unless they have had one. To me, it is so very important to discuss them because NDEs are the only accounts of what the afterlife may be like from people who actually had glimpses of it and came back to tell us of their experiences. It is kind of the halfway house between living and the afterlife and we can learn much from these accounts.

So, what exactly is an NDE?

There seem to be two distinct ways of looking at it. One is the scientific route that suggests that NDEs are simply the brain shutting down as chemicals that run it dry up. This way has no concern for any spiritual experience. It is simply the reporting of what we know about the brain by studying it as it dies and theorising that this is what causes the images and emotions of the near-death experience. In this way of explaining, these images are seen as the hallucinations of a dying physical entity - the brain. The other route of understanding is the supernatural one. This suggests that the NDE is the actual spiritual journey of the consciousness or soul as it leaves the dying body to travel to a new realm or dimension. In the supernatural explanation, the hallucinations of science are seen as visions of the afterlife.

NDEs happen in all cultures, religions, and races. What is reported follows very similar lines apart from details like what deities may be seen when in the new realms. Most people who have NDEs go into cardiac arrest as a result of disease or trauma. Their heart stops and medics or first aiders start resuscitation. Sometimes the person is not in a clinical situation and has no one about but their heart starts beating again.

The common themes of NDEs are-

The person dies and looks down on their body from either high up or across the room. They can see and hear what is happening to their bodies and can report things they shouldn't have known if they were not in a conscious state. This can range from repeating accurately what a surgeon or doctor has said. It can be information on what family members were there and what they were wearing or where they were praying. It can be as accurate as reporting the time on the clock in the ER. The person can sometimes receive a backward look at their life and a sense of their rights and wrongs.

They don't feel an attachment to their bodies, neither sadness nor fear. They simply observe. Some people also see a light or a tunnel shape with light at the end. This light is almost irresistible in its brightness and love energy. For some, this is where the NDE ends and they spiral back into their bodies as their hearts start beating again.

For others, the experience takes them through the light into a place of wonderful love and illumination. Some describe it as a verdant garden, some as simply bright clouds or the most brilliant bright light imaginable. Some say they feel like an energy of unconditional love envelopes them and they feel contentment like never before. In some cases, loved ones who have gone over before are there to greet the dying person and help them over. Sometimes it can be people that have never been known to the person in life e.g. a miscarried sibling, a great grandmother, or even a family pet. Some describe a spirit guide who comes to impart knowledge.

Some folk report great feelings of acceptance and forgiveness. They feel as though a great weight has been lifted from them. They seem to experience a consciousness that we, here on earth, could not comprehend. Some come back immensely changed by this although they can't explain why or tell us in our limited language what this consciousness was or is. Most people who have an NDE change their lives in some way massively after it. The mundane, materialistic world is never enough for them. They seek out their life purpose and pursue it with a passion never felt before. Thus, some become unacceptable to their families or spouses as they have changed too much from the person they once were. Yet they will never go back to the way they were before.

One thing that seems to differ in NDE stories is the deities that may be experienced beyond the light or in the light. This seems to be dependent on your belief here on earth. If you have been Christian you may see Jesus or the Virgin Mary. If you are Hindu you may see Hindu deities. If you are Pagan then you may see Pagan deities. If you have no particular belief you may simply see no deities at all but will still feel the intensity of the creator/source energy. Even confirmed atheists have been known to come back committed to the idea of 'something bigger than us.'

> *"Death - the last sleep? No, it is the final awakening."*
> Walter Scott

Most NDEs end with either the consciousness tumbling quickly back into the resuscitated body or with the person being told that now isn't their time or that they can make the choice to go back and finish something off in their earth life. We only hear from those who decided to come back, obviously.

So...science or paranormal or maybe a mix of both? Neither theory can be proven as yet. I know which one I adhere to and am thankful for those who are courageous enough to tell their NDE stories so we can have a glimpse of the afterlife while we are still living this life.

Below are some stories I have been graciously given about NDEs. Thank you Rachel, TJ, Shona, and Colette From Canada.

"I became very ill after consuming custard that I had left to cool on the counter overnight. My male friend had to call the ambulance because I had uncontrollable vomiting. I was in a semi-coma by the time I arrived at the emergency department. I could hear the doctor's voice, but no one could hear me trying to speak. I was aware that my blood pressure was being taken several times.

During the night I heard a big swoosh and saw a very bright twirling light in a very long bright tunnel, but it never reached the end of it."

Rachel

"When I was twenty I was diagnosed with Crohn's disease, an extremely rare form of it. Oral medication would not work, so I was hospitalised for most of my twentieth year. Shortly after turning twenty-one, during one of my hospital stays, my entire large intestines ruptured. By the time they got me up to the OR, I was already flat-lined and stayed that way for two minutes until they were able to get my heart beating again. In those two minutes, it felt like a lifetime. I remembered looking down on my body, as the surgeons frantically tried saving my life, and then in a nanosecond, was surrounded by white light. The pain I was in had been excruciating and beyond description, and had been so for months, but now it was completely gone, replaced with an indescribable sensation of pure joy, happiness, love, and every other wonderful positive emotion you could imagine. Then I saw a man approach from a distance. There was no discernible floor walls or ceiling, but I was standing on something firm, I just couldn't see what it was. As the man got closer I realised it was my grandpa that passed away when I was only eight years old. I simply could not believe my eyes, until it dawned on me that I was dead, and in heaven. He walked over to me and without saying a word we embraced for what felt like an eternity. All I remember is such an immense feeling of love and joy, as I bawled my eyes out, with happy tears. But then he looked down at me (I'm only 5'11", he was 6'4"), with sad eyes, and told me that I had to go back because it wasn't my time to be there. He told me this was just a preview of what was yet to come. I did not want to go back, I had never felt that good in my life, and knowing I was going back into a body that had just died, I knew I would be in a ton of pain. Unfortunately, it was not my choice, only the Lord himself decides that, and in a second I was back in my body waking up in the recovery room. Of course, nobody believed my story, and the doctors tried to explain it away by saying it was just the effects of lack of oxygen to the brain when I was dead, but I knew it was real. From that point on, my psychic abilities came back with a vengeance, and well for the first time in my life I'm not afraid of them anymore."

TJ

"In the Spring of 1965, my dad suffered a second heart attack and again was hospitalised in Timmins, Ontario, Canada. I remember my sisters, my mom, and myself surrounding his bed as he was in an oxygen tent. He looked so pale, so blue, so weak, so gaunt, so fragile...I was afraid that he would die...I kept writing messages on pieces of paper like: "Stay with us... Do not leave us... You have not seen any of your daughters get married, have children...choose a career...We need you!" One morning we were awakened around 5am. The nurse told my mom, my dad was on his last breath and if we wanted to say our goodbyes we should come immediately to the hospital. We rushed there from home, in Timmins to the hospital. When we arrived, we were not allowed in my dad's room as he had arrested. The crash team was with him. It seemed like an eternity. We could peek from the hospital hallway and we saw how much effort the hospital team was putting to bring him back to life. A head nurse came out to inform us he had a massive heart attack and he just passed away...Our screams were deafening...I remember just holding my mom, she had a catatonic hold on me, and she did not let go...The nursing team had left the room, and one person was disconnecting his tubes... And getting him ready for us to go see him, when the staff, by his bedside screamed, "He's got a pulse!" She pressed the call button and the whole team returned. I could see through the corner of my eye, my dad moving, eyes closed but he was coughing. The nursing staff reconnected him to various tubes and put him under the oxygen tent, which was see-through. It seemed like an eternity but thirty minutes later he opened his eyes and said, "Bonjour." I remember the twinkle in his eyes and how peaceful his demeanour was when he greeted us by his bedside. When he was a little stronger and able to speak he told me, "I went to heaven. It is amazing! The light, the warmth, the serenity - the staircase going to heaven." Dad told me who was waiting to greet him: God, Arch Angel, his dad, his sister Berthe, Napoleon Bonaparte, the French military and political leader, and our mom's mom, Eleonore. My dad wanted to keep climbing the stairs, but a warm, firm, and gentle voice told my dad that his work on earth was not done. He had to return to his family and prepare us for the future. From that moment on, my dad had no fear of dying and his heart was aching to go back to heaven."

Colette From Canada

"During my nursing career, I had several experiences with patients who always said their mother, father, wife, or a close relative was in the room with them, usually before they died. On one occasion we had a man who had a cardiac arrest and was resuscitated. When he came round he looked at me and asked, "Are you an angel?" It did make me laugh, I said no. Days later he asked to speak to me and told me that when he had died he had travelled towards a white light. He had met his mother and father but was told it wasn't his time and he had to go back. He lived for many years after that and he often popped in to see me. He changed his life from quitting a high-pressure job to spending lots of time with his family and had no fear of death. This experience of near-death was common when patients were resuscitated, not a lot spoke about it but the ones that did had very similar stories. Some patients could even tell you who stood around their bed and what was said."

Shona

The Soul Leaves the Body

*"We are born from a quiet sleep,
and we die to a calm awakening."*
Zhuangzi

I have never actually been afraid of my death. That may seem quite egotistical and even problematic, but it is just the way I have always been. When I think of my death, my pain and anguish are for leaving my loved ones and for their pain and anguish of me leaving them. Even as a little girl I had the sense that there was something more out there. I saw spirits and was always aware of the spirit world around me. So why would I be afraid?

When people say they are afraid of death I believe they are more afraid of the process of dying. It is only natural to fear a painful death or a long-drawn-out death. The process of the body dying is at its simplest, the ending of one cycle. We can understand this but still feel fearful of the process particularly if there is a disease process that is painful, debilitating, and can take away the dignity of the person. I am sure we all hope to die naturally without trauma. I believe the fear of dying also encapsulates the fear of being parted from those we love and the fear of never seeing them again. These fears are all very valid.

I have been honoured to have an experience that left me in such awe of death that I truly have no fear of the process of crossing over from our earth plane to the world of spirit. It was even more intense because I was pregnant with my second child at the time. I saw a soul leave a body as I prepared to give birth to a new soul.

I had an asthma attack when I was thirty-six weeks pregnant. I had been taken by ambulance to the local hospital and was put in a medical ward. After being given some medication and oxygen I started to feel well again but they decided to keep me in overnight. The lady in the bed next to me was from the same town and we chatted until visiting hour. She was called Mrs. Brodie, was in her sixties and so very friendly. She was recovering from bronchitis and pneumonia. Her husband had been visiting her every day and at this visiting hour, he was given the good news that she would be home in the morning. They were such a lovely couple. You could see he was lost and broken while she was in the hospital.

We settled down after visiting hour and we chatted about life and babies and husbands and how we both wanted to go home. After a cup of tea and some toast, we tried to sleep. Mrs. Brodie was very much looking forward to going home the next day. I was sleeping on my side facing her bed and she was sleeping propped up on her back. The ward was quiet as people settled down to sleep and the nurses got on with handing over to the night staff at the nursing station. My gaze was drawn to Mrs. Brodie's outline which was sparkling like a silver thread. The thread seemed made up of little sparkles and lights and it became so bright, so silvery, so unbelievably beautiful that I could not take my eyes off it.

The silver thread outline started to rise above Mrs. Brodie's body, keeping its shape and I saw it was attached to her tummy like an umbilical cord. Then the outline of silver floated up to the ceiling still connected to her physical body by the cord. I watched it all happen not knowing precisely what I was seeing. The body's outline was like a helium balloon bouncing off the ceiling with its string tied to the bed. And then the cord broke, and the silver outline was free from its mooring and it disappeared up and through the ceiling. It was only then that it became clear to me that I had seen Mrs. Brodie's soul leave her body. A nurse was passing by and I said, "Mrs. Brodie has just died." The nurse looked at me as though I was crazy because it had only been minutes ago that Mrs. Brodie was gently resting and looking forward to going home. However, when she checked her she pulled the curtains and walked quickly to get help. Doctors and nurses tried to resuscitate Mrs. Brodie. I knew in my heart that she was not coming back. The cord between her physical body and her soul body had been broken. She had gone home.

Seeing Mrs. Brodie's soul go forward on its new journey changed me forever. It was gentle, holy, sacred and most of all, joyful. It reminded me of the feelings I had when I was a nursing assistant during my university holidays. I was in a geriatric ward which was hard going as death was a constant companion. This was the place where I saw death most weeks and even at age eighteen I could sit with someone who had no relatives with them, hold their hand and simply be with them as they passed over. Never once did I see it anything less than peaceful and normal at the end. Old women and men who were shrunken and debilitated in both body and mind looked calm and serene as the pure light energy filled the room and they took their last breaths which were normally just like every other breath.

Of course, these were natural deaths of older people whose bodies were used up and debilitated. They were peaceful and gentle and seemed, well, natural. They were good deaths.

The Spirits Gather

Mrs. Brodie passed in her sleep. It was gentle and peaceful. I am sure her spirits waited for her and took her over. There are many stories about how spirits gather and are seen by someone who is in the dying process for a much longer time. These are the deaths that are due to terminal illness or non-recovery after an accident. The dying process starts long before the actual death and can be a very healing time for the person who is dying and for those who are around them at the time. The dying person will sometimes talk of having been visited by someone who has already passed. These visitations can be of a parent or a beloved grandparent, sibling, or even a treasured pet. When they pass this information on to their family members it can be a wonderfully uplifting experience. Knowing that your loved one is preparing to pass into spirit is devastating, but to know that the people they have loved wait for them and will help them safely on their journey can be such a salve.

Of course, these visitations could be scientifically seen to be hallucinations as the body slows its functions down and the brain becomes dehydrated and chemically imbalanced. This is definitely a consideration. Yet, the anecdotal evidence courtesy of the stories that follow, to me, suggests that something bigger is at play and that we do have company as we prepare to pass. There are also accounts by nursing staff who sense that something sacred is happening. My own experiences as a geriatric nursing auxiliary during my university summer holidays left me with total awe of end of life and how it simply wasn't 'chemical'. The broken, worn-out bodies and the confused, demented minds found a place of rest within as they moved towards their last hours. The rooms became hushed and a sacred, respected place and the nurses went about their business in an unhurried way. This was the time when the process of dying was honoured simply by a kind word, a soothing touch, or a change of position to bring physical comfort. Sometimes a nurse would sit with a dying patient after her shift was over or stay on to comfort the family left behind. Most nursing staff who have been a part of a patient's dying process will have a story to tell of some sort of supernatural influence.

As Shona, a former cardiac care nurse says-

"I nursed for several years in coronary care so I saw life and death most days. My parents died when I was in my teens so death and being with the dying does not frighten me. It is a privilege to be with someone as they pass."

There are also many, many stories of the dying talking to family spirits and also of relatives at the bedside sensing that there are spirits in the room. I hope you enjoy the stories below and I thank everyone who shared these precious moments with us.

"When my Norwegian dad died I sat with him. And it was a precious spiritual experience for me. My dear dad said a couple of days before he went that he had a visit from his mother and his brother. They just wanted to say they were there for him. The next day my dad said he was so glad he had already packed his suitcases because he had just spoken with his mum over the phone and they will be here to get him tomorrow. Sure enough, he died ever so peacefully the next day. And me sitting next to him felt, I have no words for what I felt, it was holy.

Love. Joy. Peace." Ragnhild

"My brother died in 2011 of cancer. The time spent with him during his illness was one of the best times of my life. We spoke about everything - sorting out the universe. One day he said he was going to tell me something and if I told anyone what he had said he would blame the drugs (he had a brilliant sense of humour.) Anyway, he told me that our father had been to visit, he said he knew he didn't have much time left but he wanted me to know that I was right as people do come to you to provide comfort and guidance. He had always doubted me about my father's words the night he died. When I said I knew they did, that it had happened so many times with people that I have sat with when they pass, he asked me to make sure I would be with him and not to leave him alone. Well, that was an easy promise as he was stuck with me no matter what. He died peacefully a few weeks later surrounded by his family. Before he became unresponsive he looked at me and told me 'they are all here' and when I asked who, he said, mum, dad, family & friends. I was so happy for him; the sadness was for my loss."

Shona

"My mother was present at both my aunt and my granny's passings. She describes my granny as having seen those coming to collect her. She smiled, reaching out to them. Asked Mom if she could see them. It was peaceful and beautiful in her eyes. My aunt was quiet as if sleeping. Just took a deep breath and passed."

Tina Turner

"Lina's experience with Heaven happened with her mother-in-law Mrs. Crawford. She called her Nana. A quote from Lina, "We had so many conversations over the years about life after death. She just found it so hard to believe. When she was on her death bed, I said to her, "Nana, could you try to give me a message from the other side that there really is a Heaven if you can?" She heard me and smiled. That night, I told her I was too tired to stay up with her but I would be sleeping in the next room and her two sons, Barry and Glen, were going home for the night. At 4am I was suddenly awoken by light pressure over my heart. I shot out of bed, ran to check on Nana and this is what I saw: she had a sweet smile, wonder in her eyes, her body was warm and she was breathing out her last gentle breaths. The whole room felt like it was full of Angels or Spirits. I'll never forget my experience. I'm sure her Spirit had just left her body and she came to wake me so I would see her happiness the moment she saw her Proof of Heaven!"

Colette from Canada

"My mum was a natural medium but never developed due to fear of what it might bring. She had a life-limiting condition and was very afraid of death. Her end came sooner than we had hoped. We all clustered around her hospital bed as she lay unconscious. I had done some development work with a medium earlier in the year and am so glad I did because I was able to link into her to find out where she was. When I saw stars and planets in a dark night sky, I knew that she had connected with the universe and had gone beyond us. That was in the early afternoon although her final breath came in the early hours of the following morning. I had told her that her dad would come for her. Someone always comes. As someone who has been privileged to give end of life care, I know that. I could feel the energy in the room and knew that they had come. Later my elder daughter told me she could hear people whispering in the room. My younger daughter saw a queue of people waiting for mum. First in the queue was a man she knew to be my mother's father. He was killed in an accident in the London fog in 1952, so she had only seen him in photographs. Not only had he come, but he was first in the queue."

Sylvie

"My grandad "Grand" was diagnosed with prostate cancer in 2000. Thereafter two other kinds of cancer; the last in his adrenal gland. Up until June/July last year, he was doing okay, slowing down but still doing bits. The pain was mostly under control. Then things took a downward spiral. In August he was confined to upstairs. Pain management becomes more difficult. My gran, Mammar, had had health issues of her own over the years. In September of last year, she was taken into hospital with suspected pancreatitis. Before we were transferred from one hospital to another she told me she wouldn't be coming home and where to find her purse with the funeral money for her and my Grand. Weeks previously she said she didn't want to be without my Grand. So, I believe this was her way out. She passed ten days later on September 24th, 2017. When she passed my Grand had already started to talk to and see people, other than us in his room. His eyes used to follow whatever he was looking at around the room. (I should say that he had "all his faculties" as he liked to say right up to this point.) He was one of twelve children, and one of the only three remaining, he was clearly using their names whilst talking to them in terms of, 'I haven't seen you for a long time what are you doing here?'

The last two days the room was calm but the atmosphere was vibrant. One evening the three of us were sitting next to his bed when simultaneously both of my aunts jumped in the air, which was funny in hindsight, but both said a small animal had brushed against their legs startling them. They both saw orbs of different colours over the last few days and I could hear what sounded like muffled conversations when the only people in the house were in the room. He passed on November 7th, just weeks really after my Mammar. My uncle was sitting with him when he passed and I'm certain he waited until my aunts weren't with him until he left us."

Jo

"One day, as I was finishing up my readings in Blessed Bee, Jim came in and closed the door. He told me that Mhairi had died that morning of a heart attack. It was such an impossible thought that I asked him, "Mhairi who?" not taking in that it could possibly be my friend. The part of Mhairi's story that is inspiring is actually around her death. She collapsed and her husband held her as she faded. She told him she loved him and then she looked right over his shoulder, smiled, and said one word, "Mum!" Then she died. I know this will give so much comfort to those of you who have lost a parent. Mhairi loved her mum so much and in the end, it was her mum who came to take her home."

Colette Clairvoyant

"My father died in 1981, I was sixteen at the time. He had heart problems and the night he died I was sitting with him waiting on the ambulance. He told me not to worry and to look after my mum as he would not be coming home. When I asked him why, he told me his mother was in the room with us. He was so comforted by this which in turn gave me peace. How wonderful to know that someone you love and loves you is waiting to help you pass. He died that night."

Shona

Here are two incidences where animals knew or sensed what was happening when someone was passing to the spirit world.

"My husband Jim told his family that, "the cat with nine lives had reached his termination day." He prepared everyone for his passing to the Afterlife and said goodbye. I was there, our two sons and their wives, our grandsons, and our granddaughter, and his two service dogs. Shep the golden retriever had his head resting on Jim's left hand and Captain Daisy, his hearing alert dog, was at his left foot on the hospital bed looking at his master. Jim told us he was heading to the Spirit World and a world without pain and he wanted us to focus on our lives, our path, our journey, and he would be by our sides. Then he went into unconscious mode, very peaceful, and we could hear his breath in and out for seven hours. At 10am on May 8th, 2014 he took his last breath. His canine companions knew right away. Shep followed Jim's Spirit out of the room and Captain Daisy turned her back to him and jumped off the bed. My sons and I did not realise it because we were anticipating another breath. My youngest son David said, "Mom do you think that was Dad's last breath?" And so we all went closer anticipating again another breath. We were hoping beyond hope. Then Ian my eldest said, "The dogs knew....they left dad's side because his Spirit is not there....and Shep followed his Spirit out the door."

Colette from Canada

"My dad Bill (eighty-seven) passed away after a long seven-year battle with bowel cancer. He had a good fulfilled life and was with my stepmother Liz for thirty-five great years. Liz who doesn't keep too well herself was in autopilot sorting out everything but it was becoming really difficult but she wouldn't hear about my Dad going in a hospice as she wanted to care for him at home and my God she did and we owe her so much. So, a hospital bed was put in place in the home and it did help but Dad was just fading away. Liz and I at separate times had said to my Dad if he wanted to go he should. I promised to look after Liz and if he wanted to go, that it was okay.

Anyway, the night before Dad passed Liz and I were sorting things in his room before we settled ourselves for the night ahead when suddenly one of their Yorkshire terrier dogs started growling, barking, running under the bed and staring at the open bedroom door, and at that exact time, I felt as though everything had stopped although I could hear the dog barking and hear Liz speaking it was muffled - I couldn't make her out. It was if I froze on the spot. Then at the open door a thick white mist that turned into beautiful staircase appeared and at the top three figures made out of the same beautiful mist were standing and I knew, I'm not sure how, but I knew it was my grandparents and my sister. They started ascending then stepped off a very large step at the bottom and headed towards my dad. You could feel the immense love and I was not one bit scared. The dog went crazy barking and the noise brought me back into the room. I felt so calm and peaceful and loved - it was truly amazing. I told my stepmum but she didn't see it, she was mesmerised by the dog's antics. The next morning at 9.05am my dad passed away, but we knew he was being looked after."

Ruby Moore

I have also heard of many dying people who know they are going but wait until they are alone. This can be frustrating for family members who have maybe sat for days with their loved one, only for them to pass when they nipped out for a bathroom break or to eat. They ask me why? All I can say is that some people are private in death as in life. They may simply want to take their last breath or let go when they are alone. They may also not want to be remembered in death but, rather, alive and vibrant. They may also feel that a sensitive soul may be overwrought and not be in the frame of mind to participate. Whatever the reason, it always comes from a good place.

Like Kristen explains below, a dying person may wait for a loved one to arrive to say goodbye to them, then choose to die when they leave the room. -

"I've worked in ICU, intensive care, and have witnessed many patients pass. A lot of them wait for a specific person to arrive and then they pass shortly after. A young man in his early thirties took some cocaine that was laced with fentanyl. By the time he got to us he was brain dead but his heart was beating. We put him on a ventilator. He was in hospital for nearly two weeks without a change. There was fighting between his wife and his family about what to do. They had decided to do minimal treatment and see what happened, and they'd be back the next day to decide further.

That night his mother came, who hadn't seen him yet and we could hear her crying from outside the room. A few hours after she left, he passed gently."

Kristen

I believe we are never alone when we pass. Even the loneliest person on earth with no real connection to their family will still have a spirit's hand to hold as they go over towards the light. This can be a family member who has recognised that they were lacking in the earth life, a childhood friend, a beloved pet, or an angel or supernatural being.

The Afterlife

"You only need to be a good person to be where I am now."
Robert Ferrie (Colette's Dad)
from the Afterlife.

What does the afterlife look like? What does it feel like? How does the soul go from living on earth to being in the afterlife? Does the afterlife exist, or do we just cease to be? Will I see my family and pets in the afterlife? I have been asked so many questions in my time as a medium and the answer is that, as yet, we have no scientific proof of an afterlife or soul progression. The only real scientific fact is that energy is never lost, it transforms into something else. So, any answer on the afterlife becomes part of belief or of listening to anecdotal experiences, either near-death or from mediums or shamans. Of course, many of us have experiences of our spirits visiting us in dreams or appearing to us, and these too, should not be discounted as, though not scientific, can hold some indication of what is beyond the veil.

Any experiences I have had with the afterlife either via mediumship or studying NDEs or simply listening to peoples' stories can only inform me. There is no proof to offer you, but I can share what I have seen, what I know, and what I believe. Of course, these experiences are explained within the limitations of my own human brain which cannot understand anything out-with our three-dimensional, linear time-line, life. What can be said, is that experiences and stories of the afterlife show many similar themes and considerable overlap. These themes are across cultures, languages, and time. They straddle world religions and are remarkably interchangeable if you exclude dogma or man-made laws that distract us from fully believing that we do not need an intermediary. The stories of the afterlife are a bit like bread making recipes. Each culture will make bread in different ways according to the recipe of what is available in each circumstance but nevertheless - the result is still 'bread'.

Near-death experiences tell of initially standing outside our bodies and viewing ourselves and understanding that we are dying or are dead, before being drawn towards a bright light. There is a sense of either our family spirits being either in this light or that they have come forth to lead us into the light. The light becomes almost blissful and draws us to it like moths to a flame. We are encompassed by it and our earth lives and the pull of what we knew becomes dim compared to the essence of the light. Once into the light, there are some reports of being transported via a tunnel or vortex at a rapid pace towards the place that holds our spiritual destination. All this happens as the energy and memory of our physical bodies recedes and is replaced by new knowledge of our souls' journey from now on towards Source. At the end of the tunnel journey, there is the place where we meet with family, masters, saints, or god. This is where the near-death experiences halt when a soul can be told 'it is not the time' and return to the body. Visiting this entrance to the afterlife can be life-changing and most people are never the same again.

The entrance to the afterlife seems to be different depending on the path or religions that have been followed, or not, here on earth. A Christian will go to the idea of a Christian heaven, with Jesus and angels. A Hindu may go to the places of Hindu gods and goddesses, a Pagan may meet with Pagan deities and so on. This familiarity makes the afterlife process easier and more understandable to the 'vibration' we are at, in this part of our soul journey. Some people see these places as where we are judged, and it is decided whether we got to heaven or hell. I see it as a place where we can experience some of what is to come before we start the healing/transition process fully. Neil Gaiman showed us his understanding of it quite brilliantly in his book 'American Gods'. Those of one faith went to 'their' understanding of heaven. The poor atheists went to a blank desert with nothing in it because that is what they believed in when on earth. This initial experience of potential bliss within what we knew and practised on earth could be what Jesus talked about when he said,

"There are "many mansions" in heaven."
John 14:2

These heavens are all shards of the same prism. My dad was a very staunch Catholic but he understood that one faith couldn't be the only faith. He had spent time in India and learned about the gods and goddesses of the Hindu faith and loved and respected his Indian friends. He used to tell a wee joke that poked fun at himself and the extremes of his faith. He spoke of when a Christian man went to heaven - he was shown around by St. Peter and saw all the different faiths all revering their particular god. He was shown The Jewish heaven, The Christian heaven, The Hindu heaven, The Muslim heaven and took it all in with delight. As they moved through the heavens, they came to a great wall. Sounds of hymns and prayers rose from behind the wall and the man asked St. Peter what the wall was there for? St. Peter put his finger to his lips and said, "Be very quiet. Behind that wall are the Catholics and they think they are the only ones here." My dad found this funny. No doubt the same self-deprecating joke could be told about many faiths or factions of faiths.

A few years after my dad died, he came back and said this to me, "You only need to be a good person to be where I am now."

This reassured me that my beliefs and thoughts regarding the afterlife were correct. This place of 'being' shows your heaven then delivers us back to whatever vibration that our soul needs to be in so that it can heal and bit by bit move back towards Source. This moving back to our relevant vibration after experiencing a higher level is what I believe the original 'purgatory' that I was taught I was going to, simply because I was human and had original sin, represented. However, it was presented in a very scary way- purgatory was just one step above Hell. I believe it was simply that having experienced the potential for total bliss that we are then pulled back from it until we are ready to join or become one with it. So, we go back to the healing place where we leave behind our earthly experiences and heavy vibration.

The way I have seen the progress through spirit is confusing because it has levels of energy and levels of spiritual development that are hard to envisage in our linear world. It is a multidimensional, multi time-line movement of which I have only had glimpses or been shown by my spirit guide, White Storm. Truly, I don't believe the individual levels are set or understandable, but I will do what I can to explain them. Please know that what I say comes only from my own experience, but many others have similar experiences although the levels are named or experienced differently.

To make it simple, imagine that we are on the ground/first floor of a seven-story building. We can only go up a level or floor once we match the energy of that floor. You have free will though and can intrinsically affect your pace or how long you take to evolve to the next level/floor depending on how much you want to elevate your vibration. The levels are as follows:

Level 1. The soul is resident in human form and living on the earth plane.

Level 2. The soul has left the body and resides in a healing place where it discards trauma, illness, and heaviness. The healing place 'time' is dependent on how the soul comes over and what it needs from this place.

Level 3. The 'Being' place. This is where we move to after our healing phase and is a place of connection with soul tribes, families, and loved ones who have passed but haven't been reincarnated. It is a place to be tutored and enlightened to the other levels of spirit.

Level 4. This is the place where souls go if they wish to be spirit guides or working spirits. This level of soul vibration is in the service of souls at lower levels.

Level 5 is the place of the higher masters. The accomplished guides can also be avatars of truth and compassion. I have also seen angels at this level.

Level 6. This is the level of Gods and Goddesses, the deities that we understand and connect to as they show us the way to Source.

Level 7 Is Source itself. Also called Great Spirit, All That Is and Holy Spirit, and many other names.

This is a mishmash of what I have seen and heard through my guide and mediumship. I can only understand it in these terms but know that it is far beyond this and far beyond my capacity to understand. It is the Great Mystery and as such, we cannot demystify it. I imagine the 'different heavens' and the levels of spirit all put in a cosmic washing machine and spun for light-years is more akin to what may actually be. Confused? It will only make sense when we individually start our afterlife journey.

My mediumship consultations have provided me with many stories from spirits that make it easier for us to comprehend the way they live on. One man who came through to his daughter indicated that his afterlife was so happy because he didn't need to buy a newspaper. He only had to think about what he wanted to know or learn, and it was available to him. She laughed at this because his head had always been in a newspaper or book when he was alive. Another man indicated that he was still free-riding on his Harley Davidson as he had been on earth. Some spirits indicate that they are working in the afterlife. Some have the 'jobs' they have always wanted or jobs that they did while alive. One man who was over a long time and had died in WW2 indicated that he was a guide who helped military men and women who were killed in service make an easy transition and move beyond the manner of their death. One woman said she had been a midwife and now helped over the babies who didn't make it to be born. One man who had grown up extremely poor and had yearned to see the ocean indicated that his soul was free, enjoying the waves and the beauty of the seas. These are ways of expressing the joy and bliss of the afterlife to us.

Different cultures and faiths have different teachings on the afterlife. These reflect the cultural norms, taboos, or even level of consciousness of that particular culture. Just as individuals can be at a higher vibration than other humans, so too can different cultures. This is general and not precise but a peace-loving, nonmaterialistic, respectful culture certainly appears to have a higher communal vibration than a gun-toting, materialistic, selfish one. Yet, I also believe that the individual soul has free will to move beyond any barriers of culture or creed.

As the departed soul moves through the afterlife in a way that we cannot fully comprehend in regard to time and dimensions, we have to work with what we have in the here and now to allow ourselves to move forward. The belief in an afterlife can help with that. Cultural or tribal ways of grieving have evolved that have been shown to work alongside the spiritual progress but in an earthy timeline. In ancient times it was believed that the soul stayed around for nine days and within that time could feast with its loved ones and celebrate its life. I have been connected with spirits who seem to wait around until after their funeral and then happily move towards their journey. Some eastern orthodox cultures have a forty-day grieving time. Within this time, the soul wanders amongst its own folk and even visits its own grave. It may fight the demons from the life it left and also have heavenly judgement as to where in the afterlife it may go. At the forty-day mark, the soul moves from the earthly plane and the ones left behind go on with life and no longer officially grieve.

Many cultures have the timing of a year in which we mourn and then move on. I have been aware that spirits tend to be able to come back and communicate after a year unless there has been something to hold them up. This can be down to the way they passed, their own free will, and also how we have processed our grief too. They will not come back unless we are ready for that mind-blowing experience. In some Native American tribes, there is the Keeping of the Soul ceremony where a trusted person is given the honour of holding space for the soul as it travels on its healing journey. The Soul Keeper is seen as someone who will not interrupt the journey with excessive grief or try to pull the soul back. They will not talk about the spirit, they will not cry or become unhinged with grief, they will stay stable and almost a barrier between the soul and the life it has left behind. This person will keep the soul's spiritual bundle and will be responsible for gifting special objects when the year of Keeping of the soul is over. Then the keeper can release their grief and be thanked for the time that they lived well, was calm and focused. It is an honoured task. The close family and friends of the soul have been gifted the time to grieve the way that they needed to without feeling guilty that they might harm the soul journey of the one they have lost.

Traditions and cultural ways of dealing with bereavement can help us move forward through our grief as the departed soul becomes familiar with the afterlife and journeys towards bliss. Remember too that these can evolve with time and progress. I consulted for a young woman who had lost her dad and I felt drawn to the ring she was wearing. I felt it was connected to her dad and maybe he had it made for her. I asked to touch it and immediately felt the essence of her dad resonating in me. I was shocked by how powerful the ring felt in connection to him. The woman laughed and cried at the same time. The ring was her dad. She and her sister had made his ashes into rings so they could feel him close every day! How amazing! A new way of dealing with grief!

Please remember this - You can only escape grief if you choose never to experience the vulnerability of love. The person we have loved is not lost to us - they have only moved into a new phase of their soul journey. We, too, will do the same in time to come. It is as natural as being born.

> *"Death and love are the two wings that bear the good man to heaven."*
> Michelangelo

Miscarriage, Termination, and IVF

"A miscarriage is a natural and common event. All told, probably more women have lost a child from this world than haven't. Most don't mention it, and they go on from day to day as if it hadn't happened, so people imagine a woman in this situation never really knew or loved what she had. But ask her sometime: how old would your child be now? And she'll know."
Barbara Kingsolver

When does the soul enter the body? We must understand this so that we can be aware of what a miscarriage is. I was brought up Roman Catholic and I was taught that the soul went into the baby at the point of fertilisation when sperm entered the egg. This is what I believed for a long time. I never really questioned that until I had my consultation business and anecdotal evidence pointed to another way. Many women would come to me for readings and as I looked at my cards I could see, for example, three children. I would say this to the woman, and she might say, "Yes I have two children and I had a miscarriage." That for me accounted for the three souls; the three children that the cards had shown.

I could also sense spirits around some of them who appeared to be young children. So, with the information from the cards and my mediumship, I could normally tell how many children a woman had conceived. So basically, children conceived and lost as a miscarriage all had a soul. This was put to the test however when early on in my consulting I read for a woman who I believed to have three children and two miscarriages. She confirmed this and was aware of the two children in spirit. I seemed to attract women to my readings who had suffered miscarriages and had sensed their babies in spirit via dreams or through other mediums.

One day a woman came to see me, and I saw in her cards that she had two children and two miscarriages. Yet I sensed more trauma around the issue of conception. I explained this to her, and she informed me that the babies who lived and the miscarriages had been conceived by IVF. She also told me that some embryos had been fertilised in a test tube and had attempted to be implanted in the womb but had come straight back through. I found this fascinating because although I could sense the souls of her children and her miscarried children, I could not sense souls in the implantation that didn't take place. She understood this and indeed it made her happy. I also did a reading for a woman who came with the question about if her embryos in the IVF lab had souls. I looked at the children that she had, and any miscarriages and it matched up to what she knew. I could not see souls in the IVF embryos that hadn't been implanted into her womb. This was an incredible solace for her.

So, in summary, fertilisation that doesn't implant for any reason does not contain a soul. Fertilisation that goes on to implant in the womb appears to have a soul even if there is a miscarriage after implantation. This is true whether an implanted foetus has two days, two weeks, or two months in the uterus. Fertilisation by IVF that is then implanted in the uterus and then attaches and goes forth as pregnancy also has a soul. Fertilised embryos that had failed at being implanted in the womb and come straight through don't appear to have a soul. Embryos stored in the medical laboratory do not have a soul. This is what has been shown to me via my readings and I believe it one hundred percent.

Where do the souls of miscarried and stillborn children go when they leave? I believe that they go straight back to Source. They haven't had to experience anything other than being in the womb and are as pure and high a vibration as can be as a human soul. They merge easily with Source, having gained the information they needed of that soul cycle. Some may go back to then come forth again in a new cycle of incarnation. Others, I believe, have used this small time on earth to fully complete their journey towards Oneness and when they go back to Source, they stay there, complete and in bliss.

This belief of the baby souls going straight back up fills me with happiness. When I lost my son to miscarriage, it was a time when many in the Catholic church encouraged the belief in the place called Limbo. Basically, and cruelly, Limbo was where babies went if they hadn't been baptised. They needed to be baptised to remove Original Sin which meant simply being human, like Adam and Eve who kind of let us all down by eating that damn apple. Babies who hadn't been baptised and miscarried or terminated babies, all went to Limbo. This was a holding place for souls who were not deemed, 'clean enough to see god.' Limbo was for eternity - an eternity of being held apart from your spirit family and your god. Yet the Church said that the babies were still eternally happy. Now imagine having miscarried a baby and the belief system you have adds insult to injury, to advise you that that longed-for baby will be in Limbo and you will never see them again. Horrific! The teaching of Limbo was to encourage quick baptism into religious dogma and was a law made by men. This was proven in 1992 when Pope Benedict XVI said that Limbo wasn't what they had said it was and could be interpreted differently, and that it was not a rule from God. Unfortunately, this wasn't well publicised, and I only read it in a magazine article years later. I had never really believed that the Jesus I knew would have such a place of torture for babies. Even the scriptures confirmed this:

"Let the little children come to me, and do not stop them; for it is to such as these that the kingdom of heaven belongs."
Matthew 19:14

I have been asked many times if a soul can leave as a miscarriage and then come back down to the same family in a subsequent pregnancy. I had always felt this was possible but not that likely until I read for a woman who had a very special little girl. The girl was about four when her mum came for a psychic reading and when I picked up on her due to her extreme psychic energy and high vibration, her mother was so pleased and said she needed to tell me something. She then went on to explain that she had been pregnant at a bad time for her family. There had been a tragedy concerning a family member that floored them. Not long after this, she had a miscarriage. She fell pregnant very soon afterward and gave birth to her present daughter, the one I had picked up on. One day her daughter started to talk about the tragedy that had happened in the past. The mum knew that she had never talked about it or the person involved, yet the child was quite emphatic about what she knew. So, the mum asked her how she knew about this? And the wonderful, psychic, gifted little daughter said, "It happened the first time I was in your tummy, mummy." I hope you have shivers because I had shivers hearing this being told. It gave me anecdotal proof that some souls do indeed come back down very quickly after they leave.

Another joy to me was the knowledge that the spirits of those we love who pass before we are pregnant get to see and know our future children first. They connect with them in Source and have interacted in ways we cannot understand. One granda spirit told his daughter not to fret about him not living to see her new baby. He said he had met her before she was conceived and that this is common for those who are part of the same soul tribe.

In all my readings where a child came back via mediumship and presented themselves to their mummy or daddy, I have never been able to tell whether that child has been miscarried or as a result of termination. This information was normally supplied by the parent. The children always just wanted to be acknowledged as what they were, sons or daughters. Some of the children showed themselves as babies. Others showed themselves at the age they would have been at the time of the reading. All were happy and delighted to be able to reconnect with their parents.

Here is the story of my miscarriage and what happened after it to show me that the soul of my child was safe.

I fell pregnant quickly in early 1992 and was very excited to be having a sibling for Jennifer. I felt very different from early on in this pregnancy and felt strongly that I was carrying a boy. Work was stressful but enjoyable. I was travelling across Glasgow every day to my branch pharmacy in the West End. (This pharmacy would be the basis of one of my novels 'The Prescription' many years later.) The fumes from the cars on the Kingston bridge made me sick every morning. In the lead up to my first scan, I had a little bleed. It wasn't much but I spotted every day after that. So, a scan was arranged, and I received the news that the baby's development was far behind what it should be. But there was a heartbeat and I hoped for the best. It was suggested that I should drop urine samples off every day on my way to work and have blood tests once a week. I felt very bloated very early on. My body seemed to be reacting to the pregnancy in a way that wasn't right.

As the weeks went along the hormone that showed the development of the baby dropped. It was discovered that I had antibodies in my blood that was killing the baby. It seems that in my first delivery that my daughter's blood had leaked into mine and set up these antibodies. Since this baby had taken my husband and daughter's blood group, I was rejecting the baby. It was a time of great sadness for me, but I felt sure that the baby could survive, and I was prepared to look after him whatever his problems would be. So, I continued the daily urine tests and weekly blood tests even though they were not offering much hope. Each afternoon I would phone the ward and ask for my results and most of the time I would be given not great news buffered with some caring words. One day I phoned for my results. I was on a break from checking medicines and my friend Janice was there helping as a dispenser as my dispenser was off ill. Thank goodness she was there. The voice I heard on the other side of the phone was huffy and almost annoyed at me asking for my results. She looked at them and said something I will remember for the rest of my life. She said, "The test results have now reached a level where the foetus is non-viable." *Non-viable?* I couldn't take it in. What did that mean? She answered that, "The foetus is non-viable. It is best if we book you in as soon as possible to remove the tissues." *Tissues?* My baby was non-viable and was now being called 'tissues'. I hung up and ran to the toilet to cry my eyes out. Janice sorted out the front shop and called my husband to come. I booked the next few days off. I don't know how I got through to the end of the day. Any prescriptions that day were checked about ten times each as my mind was so full of anguish, yet I had to work on.

The following day I was more in a fierce mood. I could not believe the words that had been used to explain that I was losing my baby. I phoned the consultant and she explained that the baby had no chance of making it to be born. I asked her if I could have a scan and she agreed. The scan was heart-breaking because it showed a very underdeveloped baby, but you could still see that it was a baby. And it had a heartbeat! I saw the consultant after it and she again suggested that I should come in right away. I told her that while my baby had a heartbeat, he was staying put inside me! She told me I was only delaying the inevitable and it was better for my health if I didn't have so many antibodies in my system. Once again, I told her that he wasn't going anywhere until he had died naturally. I had two more scans over four days. The second one didn't have a heartbeat. My baby had returned to spirit.

Something amazing happened the night after I lost my baby. I was in bed and my gran Isobel from spirit appeared at the bottom of my bed. She was holding a small baby and she said, "It's alright. I have him safe. I've called him Stuart."

This was a surprise to me as I had called him Jack! But I was so overwhelmed to know he was safe that I just cried in thanks. It took years to find out why she had chosen the name, Stuart. Her family had a secret and a baby was given up for adoption. He had been called Stuart. My mum told me this years later before she died. Seeing my wonderful gran with my baby helped me immensely. I still see Stuart a lot. He is a mischievous, playful spirit who winds up his sisters at times and demands to be included in family occasions. At first, I saw him as a baby, then as an older child. Many years later he showed himself as a young man with sandy hair and blue eyes. I know I will meet him properly when I go over to spirit myself.

Here are some heart-warming stories that have been shared for the healing potential of this book.

"My miscarriage had threatened for weeks and I had been sent home for 'nature to take its course'. It was such a sore and horrible time. I had been asked by my midwife to take a photograph of any 'tissues' so that they would know if I needed a procedure or not. Seeing the remains of my pregnancy was one of the hardest things ever. This had been my baby and I knew there had been a wee soul that had tried to make it to be with me and my husband.

My mum put the remains in a little silver ring box, and we buried it in the rockery garden with tears and prayers of gratitude for knowing Poppy, the little girl who didn't make it. This was in late February and the garden was cold and bare.

A few days later I saw a lovely plastic tulip in a shop and decided to buy it to mark Poppy's place in the rockery. The tulip was two-toned pink and red and had one curled leaf up the side. Its flower was upright and had a beautifully scalloped shape. It felt right to mark Poppy's place.

In May of the same year, I was shocked to see that one solitary tulip was growing right beside the plastic one. As it grew and opened, I realised that it was the image, in both colour and shape, of Poppy's tulip. There had never been a tulip in that spot, and we hadn't planted any bulbs. I felt this identical tulip was a recognition by Poppy of our love and her space in our lives."

Anon

"My sister-in-law and brother had a total of seven pregnancies and only two live births. My sister-in-law passed a few years ago...I was able to connect with her at her funeral. She was surrounded by all her heavenly children. She told me she was greeted by my brother (her husband - he passed many years ago) and all the children that they didn't have on earth. She said it was such a relief she had hoped and prayed to finally meet them in person. I miss her but I am joyful for her information."

Anon, Facebook

"I went to a psychic who didn't know me. She lived next door to someone I worked with and that person knew virtually nothing about me. Not very far into the reading she told me I had three children. I explained I had a stepdaughter, but she said no, this child passed early. I realised she was talking about one of my miscarriages. I'd miscarried at 13, 9, and 5 weeks. She said it would have been the child I lost at 13 weeks. I'd been unable to find out what sex the baby was at the time.

She then went on to tell me it was a boy and he was with a relative named James, who'd passed a long time ago. She then went on to say he's closest to you when you are around nature and next time you are looking at conkers on the ground thinking about picking them up just pick them up for him.

I then remembered a time when I'd been sitting on a bench in some woods, seeing some conkers, thinking about picking them up, and then changing my mind because my children were a bit older then and probably wouldn't have been interested in them.

This woman didn't know a thing about me, and she came out with that.

Also, I didn't think we had a James in the family, but I later investigated my family history and found James was my Great Grandfather."

EH

"A flower bloomed already wilting. Beginning its life with an early ending."
RJ Gonzales, Mundahlia

When A Child Dies

"Parents who have just lost a child cannot believe any words of hope. They do not want to hear them yet."
Elaine Storkey

My understanding of how deep the grief of losing a child is was heightened one day when I visited my mum in her sheltered housing a year or so before she died. She would have been seventy-two years old. I unlocked the door with my key and walked into the living room to find her crying hard. My dad had died a year earlier so I expected the tears were for him. She looked up at me with red puffy eyes and said, "I miss Isabella so much." Isabella was my sister who died of leukaemia when she was seven years old, many years before I was born. She had been dead for forty-eight years. Still, my mum grieved and was missing her little girl. My mum had gone on to have four more children and seven grandchildren. When she buried Isabella, she was already pregnant with my eldest brother Robert. Life had to go on. My mum was loved by us all and cherished by her adoring husband, my dad. I am sure that when she died both my dad and Isabella would have been there to welcome her.

My gran lost two boys, one as a toddler and the other as a young man. The toddler was kicked by a horse that pulled the milk delivery cart around the town. He was called Andrew. She lost another son when he was on training manoeuvres on the River Clyde during World War II. He was called John. I never saw photos of these boys but I knew their names and I knew how much my gran grieved for them even though she had thirteen children in all. Her grief, like my mum's, was there for life. Yet, both had to assume their responsibilities and move onward with life. My mum was happy so much of her life. My gran was a funny wee lady who was quick to laughter. Both were wounded souls.

Joe Biden, the Obama administration's Vice President, has had so much trauma in his life. His first wife and daughter were killed in a car crash in his first week as a senator. He was twenty-nine at the time. His two sons, Beau and Hunter, were injured. Years later his son Beau died of a brain tumour. He found the strength to carry on from a deep faith and that he had other children who needed him. He realised that his deep grief could help him relate to other families who had lost children. In his book 'Promise Me, Dad' he says,

"There will come a day, I promise you, when the thought of your son, or daughter, or your wife or your husband, brings a smile to your lips before it brings a tear to your eye. It will happen. My prayer for you is that day will come sooner than later."

The death of a child is almost too overwhelming to think about. I don't feel we can ever fully understand the trauma unless we have gone through it. Families and communities are rocked by the loss of a child, more than an older person. It seems out of the natural order of things. The mother of a child that was lost in my family said through tears as her coffin was carried to the hearse, "No mother should have to bury her child. It just isn't right." Everyone felt her despair from family to neighbours who had come to show their support. No one was left untouched.

My mum told me a beautiful story about the night Isabella died. They lived in a tenement building at the time that was full of families. It was 1947 and there was still rationing, and certain foods were hard to find. Isabella had fought against the leukaemia for seven weeks but was fading. She wasn't eating well but that night asked my mum if she could have an 'eggy in a cup' which was a boiled egg mashed up with butter in a teacup. My mum didn't have an egg. She asked my dad to ask the neighbours if they could spare an egg for Isabella, but no one had one that night, and no shops were open until morning. Isabella fell asleep cuddled between my mum and dad without having her egg. She passed that night. In the morning, my dad went to fetch the priest. He was holding it together for my mum until he opened the door. By now the shops were open and on the doorstep, in various wee bags, were gifts of eggs from the neighbours in the tenement. It breaks my heart every time I think of it. Yet, it shows how a child who is dying becomes precious to those that know of them.

There can also be the heartbreak of being asked if your child's organs can be donated if this is possible. I cannot begin to imagine the inner trauma that comes with that. Here, Carolyn from the USA explains what happened to her daughter and how her corneas were used to give someone sight.

"The first thing I noticed about her was her beautiful eyes. Like all newborns, they were deep blue, like the depths of the sea, and I knew they would change. I wondered what colour they would ultimately be. But there was something else. She had a complete unilateral cleft of the lip and palate on her left side. She was beautiful just the same. Her first surgery would be scheduled for around ten weeks of age. We named her October. By the time she was two her eyes were hazel, that colour somewhere between green and brown, with flecks of gold.

She was in the talented and gifted program from first through fifth grade. The last of her many surgeries was at age thirteen. In her early teens she had figured out she could make her eye colour change to very green by staring in a mirror and concentrating very hard. Right around that time she began exhibiting signs of bipolar disorder. She went through a period when she skipped school, sometimes with a friend who would provide alcohol. Later, she got involved with a guy who gave her drugs and abused her. Twice while with him, she took a full bottle of Tylenol, thinking it would kill her, but it didn't. Not then, anyway.

The overdoses did major damage to her liver, and coupled with continued use of alcohol, destroyed it. Eventually, she was diagnosed with Hepatorenal syndrome. It meant her kidneys were failing because her liver was past the point of no return. This diagnosis is not survivable. She had a horrible death. She was heavily sedated. She would arouse when they began to suction the fluid from her lungs, and she would fight like hell. I honestly cannot say for sure that she knew we were there. She struggled mightily but ultimately drowned in her own bodily fluids. We couldn't believe it. It didn't seem real. I'm not even sure I cried at that time. There has been no shortage of tears since.

In the thick of it, one of my other daughters called to say they had just gone through Portland. I had to tell her, all of them because they were all in the car together, that she was gone. They decided to come the rest of the way

I'm glad they were not there to watch her die. But there were other things to be taken care of. She had an organ donor card in her wallet. Because her organs were so badly damaged, none could be used to save some poor soul's life. But there were still her eyes. Her beautiful eyes, which had gone from midnight blue to a unique greenish brown with gold flecks by the time she was a few months old.

I was still in shock when at the hotel I got to call from the Lions Eye Bank. They were sending a representative to collect her corneas that would save the sight of someone perhaps. For a moment I tried to imagine that someone would be walking around with her beautiful eyes, but alas, corneas are not the part of the eye that has colour. At least I felt a little better, that she would be an organ donor, as was her wish, after all. She was cremated the next day."

Carolyn

Some of the saddest but also most beautiful readings I have done have been where a child comes back to reassure their parents that they are doing fine and are thriving in their spirit life. Just the proof of their name or details of how they died seem to unburden the parents and a description by the medium can bring such relief. If a child gives information on what family members are doing or relives a special memory, it is even better. A child can show themselves at the age they died or as growing up in spirit. I have seen my boy in spirit as a baby, a toddler, a teenager, and later on, as a grown man. To be reassured that your child's soul lives on and that they are happy and perfect is one of the best things that can happen.

One such life-affirming reading has always stayed with me. In one house I was reading in a child's room which was tidy and perfect with no toys out of place. I felt so many spirits around me. The mum came in for her reading and I was suddenly aware that this room had been a haven to a child who had passed into spirit. It seemed to flood with light when the mum came in. I sensed a wee girl and told her that I felt her daughter was here. Her eyes filled up and I felt her sadness. I was just about to lean forward to hug her when a little toy duck which was on a high shelf started to go 'quack, quack quack!'. The mum looked up in shock and the duck started quacking again. It was her daughter's favourite toy. I laughed and said, "Oh well something has set the duck off" and she said that it had a switch that you had to put to 'on' before the duck would quack. I was always very practical, so I said that maybe a vibration had flicked the switch. She said yes that's true. I said though that maybe it could be her daughter, and the duck quacked again! I was quite delighted for her. I was left shocked though when she told me that she had taken the batteries out of the duck a few months earlier so even if the switch had flicked, there were no batteries in it to make it quack! The wee girl was certainly a strong spirit.

So where does a child go when their soul leaves their body? They are helped over by close relatives and maybe even pets they have loved. From the moment the light opens up to them they have no fear at all. This is because they are not that long away from Source. In my experience, they do not spend much time in the healing place, if at all. They return to a soul vibration energy that isn't forgotten to them. For this reason, they also seem to be able to come back with comforting messages sooner than someone who died when old. I also believe that they can move between levels of spirit easier and can be reincarnated sooner if that is their desire. Some souls that pass as children only need the life they experienced for them to complete the final part of their soul journey.

October was a child that showed her mum Carolyn that she was an old soul and had already lived nearby:

"As a young child, October had developed a vast vocabulary, an uncanny sense of geography, a keen interest in architecture, and a vivid recollection of a past life. She told us her grandpa's name was Frank Lewis and he had lived in a blue craftsman house that just so happened to be along the route we usually took to Children's Orthopaedic Hospital where her speech therapist worked with her once a month. I stopped once and wrote down the address of the blue house. I called the county clerk and asked him to do an ownership search for a family named Lewis. Turns out, the original owner of the house was one Francis Lewis. Frank for short. It gave me chills."

Some parents can be consumed by the worry that their child suffered as they passed or that they were scared. It is the most common question I am asked as a medium. I have not had a child come back and say they were anything other than peaceful and supported as they passed over. I had confirmation of this in my own family too.

My first husband had a little niece called Helen who was a stunning wee thing, all blonde hair, big blue eyes, and cupid's bow mouth. She was a wee terror at times but funny and mischievous too. I had a kind of weird relationship with her. She made me laugh but at other times I found her too cheeky and sometimes didn't know whether I was allowed to say 'No' to her. I felt that Helen was cautious of me and I was cautious of her at times. My husband adored her and spent time with her when he could. One day my husband phoned me at work and said that Helen had been to the dentist and had a reaction to the anaesthetic and was very poorly in hospital. He was making his way there right away. She was eleven years old. Helen was on life support and was pronounced brain dead a few days later. The family imploded with grief. This wasn't helped by the fact that the newspapers had picked up on the story and tried to get photographs of the bereaved family. Nothing would make it better. A mother and father had lost their child. A brother had lost his sister. Grandparents had lost their granddaughter. Aunties and uncles had lost their niece. It became even worse when rumours circulated that the dentist had been responsible for another child's death just a few years previous. The post-mortem took over a week and many months later an inquiry showed that the adrenalin used to restart the wee girl's heart that was kept in the dentist's emergency cabinet had been out of date. It was negligence. Helen was the second child killed by a dentist who never learned from the first time. I was present at one of the saddest funerals I have ever experienced. I had never seen such grief etched onto a father and mother's face. Grandparents and relatives looked like they had been stabbed through their hearts. I was heartbroken for them. My husband was heartbroken. I was sad but I was an 'in-law' auntie to Helen so it would be wrong to claim this grief as my own. All I could do was try to help my husband and his parents.

One night, while Helen's body was still being held during the autopsy, her spirit appeared at the foot of my bed. I sat up and nudged my husband to wake up as Helen was here. He sat bolt upright, and I relayed what she said. She said that "She was here to talk to *him*. But he couldn't see her or hear her so I would have to *do*!" She was still the wee cheeky girl. Then she said to me, "Tell him it didn't hurt." And then she disappeared. He was in tears on hearing this because he had asked her as her life support was switched off, that if her spirit could come back, could she put his mind at rest.

Helen came back a few times and became quite protective of my children. She sometimes came with me when I went 'ghostbusting'. The last time I saw her spirit she was a very elegant young woman still with blue eyes and icy blonde hair. She left me after I split with my first husband. This was right. She had always been his niece and her place was with him and his family.

Before the split, I felt Helen around quite a lot. In fact, I owe her a major debt as I believe she saved my younger daughter Jillian's life. By 1997 I was thriving in my business offices and was enjoying my appointment diary booking months ahead. Jillian, age three, was at a nursery three days a week. One evening in the glorious summer, I left Jennifer and Jillian playing in the garden with their dad looking after them and set off for work along the motorway. Helen, who had died tragically at the dentist years earlier, used to join me in the car sometimes. She would also help out in readings especially when it was for a parent who had lost a child. She was maturing as a spirit and was more relaxed with me than when she was alive. I was looking forward to working knowing that it was a lovely summer night and my girls would be playing outside with their friends and would be put to bed by their dad while I worked.

I was halfway along the motorway when Helen, who had manifested in the passenger seat beside me, suddenly yelled 'Jillian' and promptly disappeared. I nearly crashed the car in fear. I knew that Helen would not have left like that if something hadn't been truly wrong. I took the first turn off and used my mobile phone to call home. No answer. I rang again. Still no answer. I started to do a U-turn to get back on the motorway. I phoned again. No answer. Just before I headed back home I rang home again and this time my husband answered.

I sobbed down the phone, "Is she okay? "and he said, "Yes, but I don't know how." Jillian had been on her little trike bike and had gone out of the garden onto the wee lane at the back of the houses. There were neighbours in the gardens across and they saw her pick up speed and head towards the road. We lived in a very quiet cul-de-sac with very little traffic. My neighbour said that she stood up and started to run towards Jillian on her bike, but Jillian reached the end of the pavement and her and her bike went into the path of a taxi. My neighbour said that what happened next freaked her out. Jillian's bike hit the side of the taxi and instead of going under its wheel, it bounced off the taxi, rotated, and threw her back onto the pavement. She said it was like some sort of miracle. She said that someone must have been looking after Jillian. I knew exactly who had been looking after her - Helen, her big cousin in Spirit. I will be forever in her debt.

"An angel in the book of life wrote down my baby's birth. Then whispered as she closed the book 'too beautiful for earth'."
Unknown

Suicide

*"Suicide is a permanent solution to
a temporary problem."*
Phil Donahue

Suicide is such a taboo topic. We wonder why someone would take their own life. Why life would be so unbearable or bleak, that suicide would appear to be the only answer? Maybe we have been low enough to have suicidal thoughts but have realised that the finality of suicide is not what we want. Most people I have talked to who have had suicidal thoughts seem to wish simply for relief from their problems, their darkness, or trauma. These problems can be physical, emotional, or mental. These people have also been glad that they didn't act on their thoughts as their lives had changed in ways that they could not have envisioned when in their time of despair. This is what upsets me so much about suicide- the lost potential. Yet, it is not my place to judge in any way. I can only tell you what I have observed in my mediumship readings and let other professional mediums add their insights.

In most of my mediumship readings where a spirit came back after suicide, there are a few things that stand out to me. The first is that it seems to take longer for the spirit to make their way back. I would expect to hear from a spirit approximately a year after their passing if it were a natural passing i.e. the fated time for the soul to move on via the natural ageing process or disease process and without undue trauma. Yet, the suicide spirits could take many years to come back and contact their loved ones. This made me wonder if it was more difficult for a suicide soul to navigate the levels of the afterlife.

Many spirits who passed with suicide explain that they didn't go to the healing place reserved for souls who passed naturally. Instead, they went to a place where they knew they were dead and that they felt secure but that was also a learning place for the soul that hadn't completed its natural life. We all have free will and using that will to end one's life has consequences just as using it in any other way does. Choosing to pass via suicide comes with all sorts of consequences for the soul of the person and for those left behind who may be severely traumatised. This learning space supported and nurtured the soul while they were shown the outcome of their suicide on earth - a bit like 'It's a Wonderful Life' but not on earth and not with an angel called Clarence. The suicide soul gets to feel the despair and the sadness of those left behind. They glimpse their longer-term potential - who they could have been. They are shown any future repercussions in their families like siblings taking their life or a parent pining away as life becomes unliveable. It seems that a person committing suicide while compos mentis manages to trade one set of horrors for a different set of horrors initially. They are shown that they didn't offload their burden into the universe, they passed it on to those left behind.

By admitting and dealing with the diaspora of grief that they left behind, the suicide souls start to understand and heal. I cannot remember having a suicide soul come through with a message within a year of passing. It can take years. This can be heartbreaking for the family left behind who may seek out mediums for solace when it is too early. The soul must work with the new understanding and make progress towards the next healing place where they may meet with loved ones and proceed with the process that a natural death would have instigated.

Carrie Woomer, of Carrie Intuitive, shares her understanding of the spiritual journey of someone who commits suicide. She can be contacted at carrieintuitive@gmail.com.

"The death of the body occurs, and the soul passes into a cleansing void. The void is a place of understanding that death has occurred. The length of time remaining in the void is determined by the soul's vibration level and choice.

The soul passes from the cleansing void to be greeted by loved ones on the other side. The soul experiences all the earthly effects made while being alive.

Every decision made and the cause and effects of all choices and those of whom they affected.

Then the soul prepares for ascension. The soul decides if it wants to work on healing from those earthly choices and effects before it can ascend into a higher realm. Some souls choose to remain in the earthly plain to prepare. (These are what we know as "ghosts") Some choose to ascend in a higher plane used for healing. The time frame is determined by choice.

When the preparation for ascension is complete, the soul moves into a higher realm with other ascended, higher vibration souls."

The second issue that seems to separate suicide souls from natural death souls is that in general, when they come back, they do so with a gentle, held back way that allows the bereaved person to either acknowledge or express that they are not ready for contact. In most cases, the bereaved person is delighted to hear from them. The messages passed seem to be very similar: That they are sorry for the sadness and trauma that they caused, that they have seen and experienced it all, and will do all in their power to make some amends. They send love, assure the loved one that they are okay and that they will see them again. This can be a turning point for those left behind.

Sometimes this connection does not go according to what the spirit may want though. One time I was doing a clairvoyant business reading for a woman. She said she wasn't interested in mediumship and we got down to business aspects. In the middle of this, my spirit channel opened, and a man came through who seemed to have the feeling of a suicide soul to me. As I tuned into him, I felt the worst pain ever across my abdomen and thought I would throw up. I felt like I had been sawn in half. The client looked at me as I explained my distress and that I felt there was a spirit that this feeling was coming from, she said, "Yes, that would be my first husband. He committed suicide by throwing himself in front of a train. Tell him to go away as I will never speak with him." Or words to that effect! I felt almost sorry for the spirit, but he had used his free will and she was using hers. She simply didn't want to hear whatever he had to say as she had lived with the aftermath of his passing.

Some of the saddest messages come from people who set out to commit suicide, used their free will to instigate it but then changed their mind at the last minute. They did not want to die at that last minute as life left them. Their healing time meant they had to deal with the trauma that their free will had caused and the knowledge of what could have been. In my experience, this takes even more time to make their way back with a message. (When I talk of time, it is from our perception rather than the spirits' perception. Time in the afterlife does not equate with our linear time but we have no way of understanding it while we are here on the earth plane.)

There is also the sadness of the soul who overdoses accidentally. They may not have planned to overdose; they may have just wanted respite. Yet their free will took a risk and lost. This is explained by Carrie Woomer below -

"While accidental overdose is not the same thing as suicide, the intent is what separates the two, but the outcomes are similar.

Because we have the free will of choice set by our intentions, cause, and effect always follow.

The week of my Aunt Jean's death was a chaotic one. Jean was renting a house in which the lease had expired. Jean was committed to be moved out of her house by the end of the week. The problem was that Jean did not have anywhere to move. The relationship that Jean had with her family, was fragile at best. It was difficult to consider placing Jean with them.

Jean struggled to find a solution.

On the last night of the lease, Jean still did not have an answer of where to go the next morning, or where to live.

When the depression hit hard, Jean found alcohol mixed with her hand full anti-depressants comforting. Her goal was to get a minute of peace, where she could tune the world out, and deal with life at a different time. Just a moment of peace, she asked the house. Then, filling the house with a song played on repeat, Jean laid down on the couch lit her cigarette, waiting for the effects of her medicine and wine to kick in. Her family found her the next morning.

On Friday evenings, I drove to class at my Reiki Master's house. I pulled into class one evening and saw my Aunt Jean's apparition at the border of his farm like property. I knew that she wanted to have a conversation with me, but I was not ready yet. Eventually, I knew it was time to let this topic between Jean and myself surface.

That afternoon, I took a nap. I had a dream where she showed me what really happened. She explained that she did not mean to overdose. She meant to feel better but did not wake up. She passed while her body tried to throw up the medicines. She choked and had a heart attack. In this dream, I could feel everything that she could feel, exactly the way that she could feel it. I could feel her emotions, her pain, her despair, her worry, and her fear when she knew her life was over. I could see the room, hear the music, and her surroundings as though I were her. Experiencing everything, all at once. I understood everything. I woke up crying. This was the first time that I understood that her passing was an accident and not an intentional suicide."

Carrie Woomer of Carrie Intuitive
at carrieintuitive@gmail.com

Some people have asked me if I know what happens when a person with extreme disease chooses to go to a private facility to end their life. In all honesty, I have never had a spirit in these circumstances come back so I truly cannot be certain. I would imagine that it would be the same as the other suicide spirits. They are using their free will to end their lives in advance of their assigned natural time. There are certainly blurred lines with suicide, and I am not an expert. I have questions that I would like answers to yet neither my spirit guide nor a suicide spirit has given me them. If someone uses their free will to simply stop taking prescribed medication that may keep them alive, is that suicide? Or is it simply giving them a chance at a natural death? What if someone has a death wish personality type and knows that something they do is an exceedingly high risk of death, whether that be climbing a mountain with no ropes or equipment, or another extreme sport? So many incidences that I have no direct messages on. I do trust that Source has the answer for every part of the spectrum of suicide. In the end, the process is about healing.

I understand that the sense of 'they are in a better place' which can be a comfort to those who have lost a loved one to suicide, is possibly being subverted by the anecdotal evidence of the afterlife 'void'. Yet, as many mediums have pointed out, it may be a difficult place for the soul to be for a while, but it is not similar to the mental torture on the earth plane that may have precipitated the suicide attempt. The soul eventually can move on to the healing level it aspires to be in but still carries the lesson of the pain it has left behind which loved ones have to deal with. This is quite different from the religions that teach that a suicide soul goes straight to hell without any chance of redemption.

Here are a few other stories of messages from suicide souls.

This reading was done about two years ago. A woman had two family members commit suicide, her father, and her older brother. Both came through and said some important things that matched up. One of which was there was nothing she could have done or said to stop them from killing themselves. An other - they were very sorry for all the pain that they had caused and they were very sad to watch the ripple effect of what happened after their suicide and see how much it had a terrible impact on the family and their generations. They also stated unequivocally that they were both free from their pain, they were not suffering anymore, they were not in hell, they were in heaven and that they had moved on spiritually. They were having to watch the effect of what they had done for eternity and were hoping to positively influence the family in any way they could so that the suicides would stop with them."

Anon, Facebook

"James, age 16, was a very edgy teenager. He felt like he never quite fit in anywhere. He felt like there were few others in the community who could relate to who he was as a person. He struggled with severe anxiety and depression. He was on prescribed medicines and in therapy to help him adjust to our imbalanced world. The day that James passed was unexpected. James was supposed to be at school when his mother had come home from her shopping trip to find James, hung in his bedroom closet with rope and a belt. James just wanted his struggle to end.

His family was devastated, as any family would be. James' family still felt him close and knew that James was safe and okay on the other side. Even after his passing, three years ago, the question from his family remains. Where did James go, after he died?

A few months ago, I was doing a mediumship session. He came through because his birthday was coming soon, and he wanted me to pass a message through to his Mom. He wanted to let her know that he was in a good place and wanted her to know that he loves her so much and that it was not her fault. I asked if he was still here, or was he in that higher place? He explained that when he first passed, he was scared and went into a dark nothingness space that seemed like nothing existed. No emotion, no nothing no fear, nothing. It was like a giant void. He did not feel anything there at all. This space was to allow a quick cleansing phase that allowed him (and others) to adjust knowing that they had passed from life into death the way they did and to ensure that he understood that the fear and anguish, medical issues, mentalities, etc. passed away with his old world.

The choice is presented later to move forward into a different plane. Understanding that you can pass through to another plane, but that you could only pass through to a plane with the same vibration that you ended with in the place of the void. All his family members and loved ones on the other side were there, to love him and help him to cross. James was not ready to cross all the way over yet. He was not stuck on our plane, but he was not quite over yet either. He felt like he needed to get some closure and help his family have some peace and closure from his crossing. This process helped raise his vibration and be in a place of even more peace and love. It took James a while to fully pass through this plane. James is in a place where he no longer hurts in any way. He feels pure joy and excitement in a way that did not happen in earlier existence but exists now. In this plane, James is tying up loose ends before he crosses over completely. His vibration matches the plane that he currently exists in. As his vibration increases, the plane that he enters has an increased vibration as well. Up until this conversation with James, I had heard about different dimensions and planes of existence, but I did not understand it in the way that James showed me. What is exceptional is that our free will remains after death and into the afterlife. James' choice to move out of a confused dark existence into a place of total light and understanding is beautiful."

Carrie Woomer of Carrie Intuitive
at carrieintuitive@gmail.com .

"The lady I bought my home from, her husband committed suicide. He was known for being a truly joyful person. His older sister was the only person on earth that knew he was suffering silently from depression. He still hangs around this house and still checks on his wife. He is so much happier but again, expresses remorse for leaving the world the way he did. He says he was a, "coward for doing what I did." He says he should have tried to talk to someone. He got stuck in his thoughts and never realised how badly his decision would affect his surviving loved ones. He feels responsible for every day that his wife and family suffer for his loss."

Anon, Facebook

As I was writing this chapter, I heard about the suicide of a woman from one of her colleagues. The feeling of sadness and upset is accompanied by the wish that, in some way, she would have reached out, and maybe someone could have helped her. If you are contemplating suicide, please reach out to someone you trust or to an outside agency such as the Samaritans. These feelings of despair may prove to be temporary. Life can change for the better in a second - you could meet the love of your life, get that fine job, find a new treatment for your illness, learn how to cope with a loss. Don't make a permanent decision that you will have to face up to in the afterlife. As Barack Obama says,

"To anyone out there who's hurting, it's not a sign of weakness to ask for help. It's a sign of strength."

When An Animal or Pet Dies

*"These creatures who share our lives,
who follow us with their wise gaze,
who pad silently through the hours,
and gently tame us with their trust,
where do they come from?*

*These creatures who slip through
the folds of time,
who teach us the dignity
of their silent language,
who pierce us with a glance,
where do they go?"*

Stephanie Sorrell in The Soul Life of Animals
by Hanne Jahr (Polair Publishing, London)

Sometimes the connection to our beloved pets can be the thing that first alerts us to death. Those of us lucky enough to have pets as children and teenagers know the deep love that we feel and the intense bond to that animal. Maybe the animal will become old and infirm and pass in a gentle way, aligned with the circle of life. Sometimes the animal will be cruelly taken away from us by disease or accident and this can also be a lesson in the randomness of death.

The question I'm most asked about animals is - Do they have a soul? My answer to that is of course they do. You only have to look in an animal's eyes to understand that there is a soul there. Some religions choose to believe the only man has a soul and animals and other beings have no soul. This allows for superiority, a lack of humanity, that enables animals to be treated badly and not looked after or respected. If you believe in reincarnation, then you will believe that we access life as animals as well as humans. The Native American people have a totem pole. Man is at the very bottom of the totem pole. The animals are next with birds at the top. The totem pole shows us that, in many ways, animals have so much wisdom to offer us if only we would choose to learn from them.

Animals live their lives based on instinct and intuition. If we watch them go about their day to day business we can learn so much about respect, cooperation, family tribe, and the beauty of existence. For example, by looking at bees we can see the hive mentality of all for one and one for all. The instinct of the bees and the way they strive for the survival of the hive, work together based on their particular skill set e.g. worker, drone, queen.

If we look at a pack of wolves and the order, even hierarchy, we can learn how to live as a community. When the wolf pack moves from one place to another, we imagine that the alpha male would be at the front leading. And yet most of the time they run back and forth to the end of the line to check on all their pack, so even the oldest and weakest are not left behind or lost.

So, we have a pet and we love them. They become our friends. They become family members. We enjoy our time with them, they comfort us, they become part of the family. And then they die. The depth of grief we feel when a pet dies can be overwhelming. It should be treated with respect by other people but so often we hear someone say, "I'm so upset. I know he was only a dog/cat/rabbit, but I am devastated." The grief that we feel at the loss of a precious pet can be intense and can also leave us very vulnerable

As a child, if this is the first connection to dying and death, then this can feel like the end of the world. Yet, in itself, the experience is worthwhile even if it can only slightly prepare us for the death of a gran or grandad or mum or dad.

So where did the souls of our beloved pets and animals go? We hear so often the term the Rainbow Bridge. This is the visual of our pet's soul leaving its body and walking towards its new spirit life. We imagine the pet's soul moving towards the place resembling animal heaven. They join up with their other friends and bound about together joyfully. But this is just a human way of taking comfort about the loss of our animal. A soul is a soul is a soul. The soul that has partaken in animal life has chosen to learn a lesson in that particular body or form. So, when it passes into the spirit world it does what other souls do. It can stay at the one level and visit us in the form we know. Or it can progress towards Source the way every other soul does. Sometimes we will see an animal spirit around us for a while after its passing. Sometimes they may decide to visit years down the line. The souls of animals seem to be very loyal and want to hang about us. Yet, at some point, they will still move forward on their spirit journey towards Source.

I have had many pets in my life, mostly dogs. I have loved the breed of Cavalier King Charles spaniel and had two beautiful ones in my twenties called Daniel and Donna. They had pups and we kept one called Brutus. He was quite a character. In years to come, we also had Tipi. When we moved to a home where we couldn't have a dog we had a rescue cat called Mysti. She was the most beautiful cat and also the most uppity. However, I kept dreaming of a little Cavalier who would need me. She indicated her name was Charlotte. After Mysti passed into the spirit world I yearned more and more for another pet. The dream of the little Cavalier girl called Charlotte never really went away.

One day we had to call from a Cavalier rescue service to say they had managed to rescue a six-year-old female from a puppy farm. She was not in good condition and we'd need to see the vet because she had had two litters of pups a year since she was one year old. We travelled to see her and I couldn't say no. I asked if her name was Charlotte and the rescue worker said that none of the dogs at the puppy farm had names and that they called every Cavalier bitch they saved 'Poppy'. I decided to call her Lottie short for Charlotte and she responded to this right away. She looked far older than six years of age. She had the sweetest face and gentlest energy. We were told that she had forgotten how to bark because it had never elicited a response at the puppy farm. She looked at me with knowing eyes and we took her home.

This was New Year's Eve, Eve, or Hogmanay Eve as it's known in Scotland. We brought Lottie into the house and she was immediately made a fuss off by my daughters. She just was the sweetest thing and stole our hearts right away. We fed her good food, had cuddle time sat on the couch between us as we watched television. I remember hearing a very small noise from her that was almost like a bark at the TV screen when we watched the Edward Scissorhands movie. As he moved towards the screen with his knife and scissor hands she backed away and barked. At that point, I knew we would never let her go. As the evening went on she became very tired. The rescue worker had told us that she was in menses and was having a slight bleed. As we settled down for the night, we noticed that she was bleeding and made her comfortable. My younger daughter lay on the floor beside her all night, cuddled her and talked to her. When I wakened in the morning I found her bedding to be very bloodied, so I phoned the vet and they said to come in right away. The journey to the vets is one of the worst ever. My daughter cuddled Lottie while I drove. I had such I sense of dread in my heart. This little Lottie had come into our lives for all of twenty-four hours but had stolen our hearts.

We were taken straight away at the vet's. The vet seemed very concerned, but we still hoped that something would be done to make Lottie healthy again, maybe medication. But a lovely young vet told us that Lottie was already going into shock and that she'd suffered enough. She asked us to let her go as she was suffering. We cuddled her and told her how much she meant to us and then we waited as she died. The loss felt so intense. It was New Year's Eve and in one day we had known the joy of knowing and loving Lottie and also losing her. I felt rage against the people who ran the puppy farm. They had killed a beautiful little dog simply by over-breeding her for money. We would have happily paid for her treatment, but we found ourselves paying for her cremation. There were no celebrations that New Year's Eve for our family.

Lottie imprinted herself on our souls. I'm sure she was truly part of our soul tribe. We connected so deeply to her that there is no other explanation. We had great joy within a few days when I saw her spirit in the room she had been in on her last night on this earth as a dog called Lottie. Very soon she was felt by other family members. Lottie has joined us from the spirit world on many occasions. We seem precious to her just as she is precious to us. I knew I had dreamt of her so that we could rescue her and give her the best last day of her life. Nothing would ever convince me that Lottie did not have a soul and that she was not a member of our wee soul tribe.

In my mediumship sessions on YouTube, I have had many animals come through with messages for their humans. I have had horses, dogs and cats, rabbits, and guinea pigs. I also have had birds like parrots and budgies. Some give their names. Others give the name of their human and give thanks for the relationship. Some come to say that their human had made the correct decision when they had to put them to sleep. Some confirm their presence in homes. Sometimes we see Mysti around, sometimes it's Daniel, sometimes it's Lottie. Yet I don't sense Tipi, Donna, or Brutus. So maybe the latter souls have moved on to a different level of spirit or have come back to another family in whatever form they have chosen for their new life.

"Can you imagine our planet without animals, insects, and birds? Just for a few moments contemplate what it would be like..."
From The Soul Life of Animals by Hanne Jahr (Polair Publishing, London)

Animal Messages From Over The Rainbow Bridge

So many animal lovers sent me their stories about their beloved pets. Thank you all so much. Here are some of them.

A dog who love-bombs his human from spirit…

"In 2017 my dear friend of nearly fourteen years crossed the rainbow bridge. His name was Tony, a deaf yellow lab, with some medical conditions that required plenty of nursing. We were extremely close and when I went down hard in '13, the therapy pooch in him rose and helped me through years of heavy treatments. One day, months after he died, as I was resting. I thought of him. Then I swear some part of my vision *saw* him, on his mat by the front door like the ole days, then I saw him get up and come over to me and as soon as I reached out for him, taking his big ole head close to mine I was *bombed* with a sense of intense love, the likes of which I had never known, not even close. Tears and laughter wracked me hard as I cradled and nuzzled that sweet mug into my neck and then quickly—it was over—my heart almost relieved, as that level of intensity is not sustainable, at least in this world. Just so *much* inconceivable, supernatural *joy*. I cry now remembering. Since then, more love-bombs have struck, none from dear T like that, but other cherished sources."

Juanita Grande

A story of a cat that knew when death was coming...

"Our cat Fluffy was a pretty black cat; fluffy with a little round fat face and a wonderful personality.

So back in 2003, I had back surgery and Fluffy would jump up on the bed when I was in the most awful pain and rest up against my back and purr and keep my back warm until I fell asleep. Also, in 2012 my husband passed away from cancer and Fluffy spent quite a bit of time with him leading up to his death. Another time I had a friend over and Fluffy wasn't one to come up to strangers, and this friend was never even at our house before. But she went right up to him. She was sitting on the back steps when I drove in the driveway. And as soon as he opened the car door she came down the stairs and greeted him at the car, rubbed up against him, and let him pet her. He said, "Wow what a nice cat." I said, "Thank you," and, "Wow she has never done that before she usually stays away from people she doesn't know."

Well, a sadness came the next day for my friend passed away that night. And on another occasion, she said her goodbyes once again. My mom was very breathless, and she moved in with us and was diagnosed with lung cancer in 2013. Mom wasn't feeling well one day, and she had asked me to call Hospice and for them to send an ambulance to transfer her to Hospice House. So, as we got her small suitcase together. Fluffy was near her feet and sitting ever so close and Mom was petting her and talking to her and Fluffy just looked at her as if she understood what mom was saying. The ambulance showed up and Fluffy wouldn't move - she wanted to stay with Mom and didn't want her to leave. Five days later mom passed away in 2014."

Joyce Zdovc, United States

A dog who answers to her predecessor's name…

"My mastiff was called Jessie. When she was dying, I told her to come back because I had her later in life as a rescue. I wanted her to come back as my puppy next, then a year later I ended up with a mastiff mix puppy and we called her Hallequine Star but she does stuff just like my old girl did and when you call my old dog's name she comes to it. You can see it in her eyes, always in the eyes."

Nicoletta Castle

A cat who comes back for cuddles and snuggles…

"I had the privilege to share eighteen years of my life with a total earth angel albeit a very mischievous one named Samson the Delightful (Sammy) a silver Maine Coon and wonderful, fluffy family member. He died at home of natural causes. I was beyond devastated. He had seen me through divorce, bereavement, slept with me night after night and got up to untold nonsense. He died in our living room in a box in front of his favourite open fire. My daughter was due to come home the following day. The energy around him felt like that cool energy of angels. He looked perfect and stayed perfect for her to come home, grieve for him and us to mourn. I was bereft. I longed to see him again. I was even doubting my skills as a medium. Then I was in bed and woke to his big noisy greeting and felt him snuggle into my arms. He felt soft and snuggly and just him. I thanked him so much for showing himself to me and all those years of love. I fell back to sleep. Then about six months ago I saw him in the drive, clear as day, waiting for me to come like he used to. It was three years since he had passed, and my heart skipped a beat. I know he was my healer cat sent to radiate love and I know the bridge I cross when my time comes will be a rainbow one with him waiting."

Kathy

A dream that predicted an animal's death…

"This is so weird, but I had a dream last night that my first dog came to visit me. I got home from work today and found out the dog I have now died. His heart gave out. I have dreams all the time. I think it's the way the universe lets me know what's going on. Maybe so I won't be so shocked."

Laurie

Animals who come back to their old beds…

"Last year on February 23, 2019, I put my ten-year-old male cat Ricky, down. My heart was broken. I cried and cried for days. I talked to God and Ricky every day asking for a sign that he was okay. One day I was on my way to an appointment. I picked up breakfast, sat in the car eating, still feeling down in the dumps, and asked once again for that sign. I picked up my cell phone and there was a notification of a meditation titled, "Recovering from Heartache and Loss." Imagine my surprise, what a coincidence that this would pop up during my time of grief. Of course, without hesitation, I played it that night when I got home. I was listening to this meditation with my eyes closed. Suddenly I saw this beautiful vision. It was like a white shimmery crystal. It slowly and gently floated from the right. When it got in the middle, I saw it had an eye. It gently blinked, continued to float towards the left, and disappeared. That was my sign that he was okay. Before that happened, I had never seen a vision in my entire life. I have also felt something on my legs when I have gone to bed. I feel that was Ricky coming back to visit.

Years ago, there was another cat that had passed and when I went to bed I felt the same sensation on my bed as I did when he was alive. Not too long ago a friend said to me, "You're going to think I'm nuts, but it felt like Tucson (her dog who passed) walking on the bed last night." They do live on and come back to visit."

Nancy

A rabbit who hops back every so often…

"Hopscotch, our rabbit passed away in 2012, one week after my husband. And every so often my son and I would see HopScotch in the hallway hopping around the corner, or at least a shadow of him, real quick out of the corner of our eye."

Joyce Zdovc, United States

The cat who brought sunshine…

"The last three days of Zus's life were dreadful, as she had then stopped eating and was barely drinking. Our rule was three days of no/barely eating and drinking would mean the evening of the third day having her euthanized. The second night I sat alone with her, holding her, and crying and singing her 'Love of My Life' by Queen (I get teary just thinking of the song even now). I talked to her about all the wonderful memories we had together, all her qualities that we so loved, and at last, I told her it was okay to let go if she was ready. That it was okay, and we loved her and would respect her wish. The next morning, she voraciously ate a few bites of food, but as the day went on she just got quieter. Her eyes changed. Her breathing changed. She was ready. And when the time came, I held her, she was put into a gentle soft sleep, and then went. It was very peaceful for her. For us, it was not at all peaceful. Every single one of us was distraught at her loss.

We buried her in our back garden with a gravestone and potted flowers. As I paid my respects to her at the burial, it was a rainy gloomy day. I asked Grandfather Sun to shine upon her and show her the way. And just as I prayed the sun suddenly came through the clouds, shining massive golden rays down upon her grave, and a giant rainbow appeared overhead. This experience was just beyond words, and it did help me to feel it was the right thing

A few months later I had a dream that we were able to bring my darling girl back to life, and we did. But it was horrific and not at all natural, and she was in immense pain. In this dream, we immediately regretted our choice to play with life and death and realised how selfish it was for us to wish upon her that she remains with us instead of moving on. That's when I knew absolutely that she came in dream-time to confirm with me to stop living with regret and guilt over choosing to let her go, and that she had made peace with her passing."

Kristi Janssen

A dog who showed life beyond the veil…

"Once my husband and I were waiting for someone at the front door in our house. A golden retriever dog came out of nowhere running like crazy and went straight inside our house. It was an old female dog, very sweet and pretty. She refused to go outside and kept giving me her paw. I already had two dogs and didn't know exactly what to do. Since it was late at night, we decided to think it over and decide the next morning. Well, the dog stayed. We called her Bubba and loved her very much. Months later Bubba fell sick with cancer. She developed a tumour in one of her paws. I suffered a lot. I wanted her to live and couldn't reconcile with the idea of her death. She passed the last day of the year. A couple of weeks later I had this marvellous dream, like no dream I've had before or after: It was the most beautiful landscape you can imagine, the greenest grass, the most amazing colours. And there was Bubba, once again running towards me. She came close and showed me the paw that had the tumour and said without words, "Look, mommy, I am well now, everything is alright." I embraced her by the neck. She smelled so good. There was a creek in front of us. "I will cross you over," she said and took me to the other side. I think she will come for me when I must cross to the place she is. If that happens, it would be the best gift I could receive."

Ruth Sarmiento

Cats that come back for cuddles…

"I used to work nights and when I came home and went to bed my four cats would cuddle into me. Sadly, my cats have all passed now and I am retired but I still feel my cats get on the bed and cuddle into me sometimes. It's so reassuring that our souls go on."

Jo

Is Hissy really Fluffy reincarnated..?

"Fluffy didn't care for outside animals or rather not in her territory (yard) so to speak. There was a stray/feral cat that had kittens. I fed them every morning. Those kittens grew up and the one female stuck around she was a pretty calico and I named her Callie. One of her kittens became the mother of Hissy the cat we now have that I believe Fluffy had some sort of agreement or was reincarnated.

Fluffy passed on around Father's Day 2014, and every so often at night, I would feel the foot of the bed jerk a little and footsteps as paws on my bed. I would just say, "Hello Fluffy" and roll over and go back to sleep. Fluffy and Hissy have so much in common. Here are some reasons why I feel Hissy is Fluffy reincarnated:

Fluffy when she passed limped from her right front leg; Hissy got hurt and limps right front leg too.

Fluffy was declawed. Hissy has claws but doesn't quite know how to use them, she grabs stuff and gets stuck all the time. I would have to take hold of her little paws and rub them and tell her to let go.

Fluffy wasn't allowed to eat people food. Hissy won't even try people food, she snubs it. Fluffy wouldn't go on counters, sinks table. She wasn't allowed. Hissy doesn't even try to go on counters, sinks, kitchen table, etc.

And when you talk to Hissy and ask her are you Fluffy? She looks at you and almost as if she is saying yes and mews real softly at you."

Joyce Zdovc, United States

Grief for an animal can last many years...

"My cat's name was Castor, his brother was Pollux though he got hit by a car within about a month of getting the twins. When Castor was about eleven years old his kidneys gave out. I had to have him put to sleep and cried buckets. That was about eighteen years ago. I still miss him even though I've had other cats - he was that special. Not long after he passed, I would see him out of the corner of my eye. Sometimes he would walk by and I would catch a glimpse. Sometimes I even felt him laying my lap. When my last cat Chaucer passed away last year, I didn't seem to feel him being around, and I have not seen Castor since then either. I wonder if they are together and keeping each other company."

Angela, Colorado, USA

When a dog has a spirit playmate...

"I was having medical issues and recovering from stomach surgery. One day I was walking in a field with my pup Cookie Dog and she was very active. I was talking to God and I asked God if he could send my other pup KB, that passed away years earlier, to play with her. To my surprise and joy suddenly Cookie Dog was playing with something, wagging her tail having a grand time. It looked like she was playing with some other dog. I continued my talk with God, and she had time of her life! I know KB was there. I felt her on my legs. I loved it!"

Eugene

A dog spirit that saved a life...

"My mini pinscher male named Boru lived for fourteen years. About two weeks after he passed my daughter was walking back from her grandmas after dark. (We live about a quarter-mile from her out in the country.) She suddenly heard a car - she had her headphones on even though I have told her one million times not to walk with them. She said she started to turn to see where it was when Boru jumped into her arms causing her to overbalance and fall *off* the dirt road into the ditch. At the same time, the car passed. It never slowed down. If she had been on the road she would have been hit. She got up and spent five to ten minutes trying to find Boru or a mini pinscher and came home pretty shook up."

Kathleen J from Oklahoma

Proof that animals mourn...

"We had two parakeets, Snowflake and Kenny. Snowflake had gotten a tumour on her wing. We were putting a salve and medicine on her wing and bought a small nest for the cage and kept a flashlight lit to help her stay warm. We had to separate them. But kept their cages right next to each other. Kenny would sit as close to the other cage as he could and watch her. Then one evening while eating dinner, Kenny left out a very loud squawk. This wasn't a regular chirp. It sounded as though he was crying and saying goodbye. Right away we looked at each other at the dinner table and said oh no and went upstairs, and yes, Snowflake had passed.

Time went by and we got another bird, to keep Kenny company. Kenny treated this little bird like a son; He would feed and preen him. That bird's name is Skye. And when it was time for

Kenny to join Snowflake, little Skye bird sat near the birdcage door for a day or so. I guess waiting for Kenny to come back in the cage. It's interesting how animals mourn too."

Joyce

The dog who came in a dream to say goodbye…

"My grandparents had a lovely German Shepard dog named Atos. I had a very strong bond with him. He saved my life pulling me away from a truck and I was nearly hit by a train saving his life. We've been through a lot together. On one occasion when I didn't visit my grandparents with my family, he thought something had happened to me and he stopped eating and nearly died and I had to talk to him through the phone! Only then did he start eating again. When he died everybody was scared to tell me, but I knew anyway because he came in my dream and said goodbye. I woke up with my pillow soaking wet. I still miss him badly. After, whenever I was coming home late at night alone, there was a stray white dog that came out of nowhere, just walking me home then disappearing. I like to think it's Atos still taking care of me."

Agnieszka Lellouche

A spirit dog who decided it was time for a new companion for his human…

"I waited to get another dog. It had been over two years since he had passed but having Boru for so long I honestly had to get over my grief a bit before getting another. Well, one night I again was wondering if I could go look at a rescue/pound but kind of shying away. Boru had been my dog directly after the brain aneurysm I had, he warned me about seizures, I couldn't face getting another dog and thinking less of that animal because of comparing them to Boru. I laid down to go to sleep when a movement caught my attention at the floor level. I sat up and couldn't find anything. I lay back down thinking there hadn't been any signs of mice, but something moved. I almost got to sleep when I felt a dip in the bed just like when Boru jumped onto the bed. I sat up again and turned on the light. I said aloud, "Should I go to the shelter tomorrow?" I felt a couple of licks on my foot. We went to the shelter and found a female miniature pinscher, Grania. From the moment we brought her home she was just instantly, seamlessly part of the family. She came through the front door, went to my room, waited beside the bed for me to get Boru's step stool, and bounded onto the bed. She has since jumped up on the bed without the step. I think the point she was trying to make was she knew the step stool *should* be there."

Kathleen J from Oklahoma

The message on behalf of a group on animals...

"I was recording my fortnightly Colette Clairvoyant YouTube Channel 'Messages from the Spirit World' video. I am used to having all sorts of animals coming through to thank their humans for love and joy. But on this day, I had an ostrich! They are bigger than I had imagined! The ostrich seemed annoyed, as though he had a grievance. He communicated that, yes, I was seeing him correctly and feeling his anger. He communicated that he wasn't here for himself but for ostriches as a group as they were being wiped out massively in certain areas of the world. He indicated that this couldn't continue, and I had to let humans know. I passed on his messages and was in awe of the strength of his message, as though it had the intensity of many other ostrich souls behind it too. Once the video went live I had a few people saying that certain countries were over farming ostriches for their meat. The birds were imported to countries that they weren't indigenous to and bred simply for meat. No wonder my spirit ostrich was angry."

Colette Clairvoyant.

*"Dogs come into our lives and leave
paw prints on our hearts."*
Anonymous

Bereavement and Navigating Grief

"Someday you will be faced with the reality of loss. And as life goes on, days rolling into nights, it will become clear that you never really stop missing someone special who's gone, you just learn to live around the gaping hole of their absence. When you lose someone you can't imagine living without, your heart breaks wide open, and the bad news is you never completely get over the loss. You will never forget them. However, in a backwards way, this is also good news. They will live on in the warmth of your broken heart that doesn't fully heal back up, and you will continue to grow and experience life, even with your wound. It's like badly breaking an ankle that never heals perfectly, and that still hurts when you dance, but you dance anyway with a slight limp, and this limp just adds to the depth of your performance and the authenticity of your character. The people you lose remain a part of you. Remember them and always cherish the good moments spent with them."
Christopher Walken

Grief is different for every single person. Although it can follow certain psychological ways of expression, it is a personal and very lonely journey. Each stage is specific to the person experiencing it and each moment can be a pivot either into memories of despair or memories of joy. Grief may start before a person dies. If a loved one is terminally ill, or has a terrible quality of life, or even has a condition where their essence seems to disappear with time, we can begin our grief process many years before they die. This is called anticipatory grief. This form of grief is debilitating yet is normally not easily recognised or accepted. This means the person experiencing it can feel very alone and isolated. They may not ask for help because they feel unworthy of it when their loved one is still physically present.

I remember doing a tarot reading for a woman and saw that her dad had been ill for years and had little quality of life. I also saw intense guilt in her cards, so I asked her about why she felt this. She said that on some days she wished her poor dad would die and be away from all his pain. She started to cry and explained how she must be such a bad person to be wishing that her dad would pass, even while not being able to contemplate a life without him.

I felt it was time for me to tell her my truth. I explained to her that if she was a bad person, then I must be one too. This got her attention. I told her about my wonderful dad, who had suffered nine years of strokes and had little quality of life for his last two or three years. He could not talk and needed care and attention for doing the simplest tasks in life. My dad was my rock, my cheerleader, my hero. In the days after I lost my second baby, it was to my dad I ran. He only had one working arm but, oh, he held me so tight that I felt he was trying to squeeze the pain out of my body. When both my daughters were born, everyone managed to visit the hospital except my poorly dad. The first thing I did when I was allowed home was to take my daughters to visit their loving granddad. It broke my heart that less important people had been introduced to them before he had.

I could not fathom a life without him. Yet for years before he passed, I prayed at night for a gentle angel to come and collect him and take him home. He was unhappy, very frustrated, and in pain. I raged at God for allowing this wonderful man to have such an undignified end to his life. My heart felt it could never let him go, yet my mind was strong in wishing him peace. When I explained this to my client, she felt a weight had been lifted off her. She did not see me as being a bad person, so she could accept that neither was she. She was already grieving her dad. Grieving the person he was and the person he would never be again. She was working her way, just like I had, through anticipatory grief.

This type of grief is common with physical deterioration but is also felt deeply when a loved one loses their personality, their memory, or their core values. Dementia type illnesses, where a loved one does not know who they are or who family members are, can lead to extreme anticipatory grief. You start to grieve for the person you are losing to a void rather than death. The guilt, anger, and stress that comes from this cannot be underestimated. The loved one may look well enough physically but is a thousand miles away from the person they were mentally.

I believe we should talk more about anticipatory grief. We try to support people who have been bereaved, yet we can forget that some people are already grieving for a person they are losing, or have lost, without an actual death. We would bring food and help to the recently bereaved. It would be good if we could lend our support to those who need it in advance. Also, it is worth noting that after years of anticipatory grief, the actual bereavement may still be as devastating as it would have been without it. This quote below is from someone I follow on Twitter and I believe he says it all regarding dealing with anticipatory grief.

"I think the most hurtful thing is when dealing with a parent or loved one that's dying is the expectation that the people who are trying to overcome this pain will somehow be able to function as if this weren't happening to them." Anon

The five stages of grief that are universally recognised can be felt during anticipatory grief and after a bereavement. They are based on the Kubler-Ross model. They are based on emotions felt during the transition from despair to survival. Each one can overlap the other to a degree and many of the mental and physical symptoms can be present randomly throughout the process.

The first stage is denial.

You hear of your loved one's death. You do not believe it. It simply could not have happened. You only saw them a few days ago and they were fine. The person informing you is mistaken. In fact, they may even be lying. There is no way this is happening! You may try to phone the person. You will certainly decide to visit them just to show yourself that they are still alive and well.

At the same time, your heart may be sinking in your chest. A little voice inside is trying to make you listen to the truth. You may feel dizzy. You may collapse. You may run away to be alone, so you do not need to hear what is being said. You may choose to simply go and make the dinner or feed the dog or do the laundry because what you are being told is simply not true. You may go into a state of shock.

The second stage is anger.

Once the news has sunk in and you cannot deny that it is true, there can be a truly intense feeling of anger. You may feel rage at the person who informed you of the passing. Or the people around you that are going on with their life. How dare they? Are they so unfeeling as to be able to function when you cannot? You may blame the doctor who attended the dying person. You may rage at the mistakes that you perceive may have contributed. You may be angry at yourself for words left unsaid, for previous frustrated feelings about your loved one. You may be angry at the person themselves for dying and leaving you without them. You may rage at God for taking the person away from you.

This anger can cause arguments in families. It can also be destructive in the way it comes out in bad behaviour. It can also be devastating if it is buried under alcohol, gambling, lack of inhibition, or self-harm. The anger needs to be expressed but in a safe, controlled way. Communication and grief support can be beneficial at this stage. A person may not accept counselling in the denial phase but may see it as a necessary thing in the anger phase.

The third stage is bargaining.

The bargaining stage can be more easily recognised in the lead up to the death of a person when we may bargain with a higher power for more time. We may bargain that at that time we will be better people, look after our loved ones better or even just enjoy being in the moment with them. After a bereavement, the bargaining phase is the major bridge between denial and acceptance. In this phase, we are beginning to realise that the person has gone but not yet ready to accept it. So, we bargain almost in retrospect. For example - if we had acted quicker, our loved one may have been saved or if we had prayed more or believed more then they could still be here. This is an attempt to think we could have changed the outcome in some way. In thinking in this way, we are moving towards acceptance.

You may feel the need to make bargains to relieve the pain you are feeling from your loss. This can be to a higher power in the form of prayer for some release from the pain and vulnerability that comes from losing love. You may even bargain for some sort of oblivion for a while with a promise of being back to 'normal' after it. The exhaustion of this stage may make you simply want permission to lie down and float away. Bargaining can seem so surreal but also shows that you are making progress. The more you bargain, the more your brain must accept that the person has gone. You cannot ask for someone back if you have not begun to accept that they have gone. You cannot bargain for respite from grief if you are in denial about what is causing the grief.

The fourth stage is depression

After we realise that bargaining does not achieve anything, we are on our way to a harsh reality. That reality involves an understanding that whatever we do or promise, that our loved one is not coming back, and our grief is still a major part of our life. This return to reality brings with it a sense of what life will be like without our beloved person. We understand the loneliness and vulnerability that we feel and know that it will probably be a fixture of life as we go forward. Although we are further along the road to acceptance, this fourth stage can be devastating.

You may feel the need to be alone and without the intrusion of general life. The black cloud that you feel descending may feel like it may never lift. The people who helped and were very understanding a few months ago may now have moved on with their own lives and not be as caring or supportive. You probably need them now like never before but may feel that you have asked as much of them as you deserve. You may feel worthless and that life has no meaning. Working through the depression phase with communication and self-care will allow movement to stage five.

The fifth stage is acceptance.

At one point in the depression, a light will go on. It may be the tiniest light, but it is enough for you to see and move toward. The darkness will become less dark. The heavy tiredness and despair will begin to dissipate. Life will call us back to resume truly living again. At this stage, acceptance allows us to smile at the memory of our loved one before the tears come. In fact, we may find that we can control the tears if we feel that they are inappropriate in a situation e.g. a workplace meeting. By accepting that we have truly been bereaved, we can now start the rebuilding and moving forward to a new normal where we still grieve but not all the time.

You may feel a lightness coming back to your life. You will feel more capable of making plans and being optimistic about the future. You can accept the passing of the person so can also now celebrate their life, their gifts, and the person that they were to you. You may rejoice in memories of special times. Yes, you may cry and feel vulnerable but there is a strength behind you now. You may have come through the darkness and a loss of faith but now may think of your person in the afterlife and with the knowledge that they mattered and will never be forgotten.

These five stages of grief are fluid. They can be long or short; there or not there; intense or gentle, depending on the individual. Knowing them can be helpful. Of course, they all come with physical symptoms that may be underestimated. I always tell a bereaved person not to be frustrated with the exhaustion that comes with grief. Exhaustion can be caused by crying or the headaches that can come with constant tears and stress, lack of sleep, and trying to go on with ordinary life while coping with loss. A bereaved person can feel dizziness, tiredness, muscle weakness, hunger, or lack of appetite. They can be clumsier, more accident-prone, have palpitations, and panic attacks. Normally this will pass with time. Sometimes though, the partner of the person who died can die very soon after them. There is a term called Broken Heart Syndrome where a person's heart can be damaged by the intense grief that comes with loss. We may say that they have died of a broken heart and they truly have. I have heard stories of older couples who died within minutes of one another even when they were separated by location. If the broken heart does not kill the one left behind right away, they may just go downhill and pine away. I see this more in old men who lose their wives than the other way around. My theory on this is that women will generally talk and share grief with other women and in so doing begin to heal and gather support. In general, older men do not talk about or share their grief especially as time goes on when they believe they should be stoic and have stiff upper lips. Communication and accepting support seem to be easier for women in my opinion.

How to navigate grief?

As all the stages of grief are very fluid, there is no one way to navigate bereavement. It is a personal journey. There is no right way or wrong way if you are not hurting yourself or others. People may give you leeway for being irritable and angry, but it may only lead you to guilt and sorrow for yourself later. If it does, please forgive yourself. You are not a bad person. Everyone will go through the death of a loved one. Emotions can be so raw that we might not even recognise ourselves as we go through them.

There are a few insights I can offer from my personal experience and I hope they will help.

First, I would say not to make any major life decisions while you are grieving. Your frame of mind is all wrong for major change and you may fail to carry decisions through due to exhaustion and this can lead to feelings of failure on top of the grieving process. My own experience of this was that two days after my dad died, I decided I would divorce my first husband. I had the lawyer's business card in my purse and was simply waiting until after the funeral. Two people offered me good advice - my lovely mum-in-law, who said, if you give it three months and you still want this, then I will support your decision. The lawyer I phoned asked me to wait a while before instigating proceedings because she felt my state of mind was chaotic. I took the advice and journeyed through my grief. I adapted to a new normal. And then my mum died two years later and the whole process started again. Within that time, I avoided the breakup of my family unit and the extra upheaval and even the expense of a separation. I did divorce my first husband, just not during my grieving time. The lawyer and my darling mum-in-law had been right in asking me to pause.

Upheavals that you probably don't need during the first two years after a loved one passes include moving home, divorce, a career move (I gave up pharmacy to be a clairvoyant six months after my mum died so I am preaching a wee bit here!) or debilitating illness. If these cannot be delayed, then you need to look after yourself even more. A bereaved person needs to pace themselves and nurture their health and energy. They need to have time to simply be with their thoughts and memories. Anything that distracts from that in a major way is just prolonging the grieving time. Distraction and busyness only stave off the inevitable. Grief must be worked through, not delayed by a new project, a new relationship, or alcohol or drugs. Sit quietly with your grief and let it take you where you need to go.

The second piece of advice I would give is to not expect others e.g. workmates, colleagues, retail staff or even the public to know or be aware of your grief. This aspect hit me hard three days after my dad died. I wanted to be well turned out for my dad's funeral. I would be pushing my mum in her wheelchair and would be focused on her, so I decided to get my outfit and have my hair cut all in one day. My mum-in-law came over to look after my girls and off I went. I grabbed the first black dress I could find without trying it on. Then I proceeded to go to a very local hairdresser that was non-appointment - you just turned up and waited. I gave some basic instructions to the very cheery hairdresser about trimming my shoulder-length curly red hair. I felt disinterested in the whole experience-it was simply something to get through. I zoned out and when I came back to, I had the worst short haircut of my life. I paid her and fled. As I walked into the street, your typical wee Glasgow man looked at me and said, "Cheer up darlin', it may never happen!" I turned to him like an angry Gorgon (without the hair) and shouted, "It just did. My dad died!" The poor man just about melted into the wall.

My dad had died but life in the outside world was going on. The hairdresser and the wee man did not know that I was grieving. Or the woman with the pram that ran into me when I stopped suddenly when I thought I saw my dad in the street. Or the newsagent. Or the pharmacy group area manager that I did locum work for who asked me to work my lunch hour when I was simply exhausted with grief. Generally, when people are told of your grief, they do understand and adjust. Some do not though. In circumstances like these, you do learn who has your back and who has no empathy. These can be good lessons learned. I never offered my services to that company again.

The third bit of advice I would give is to try to maintain a routine and the rituals of life. It can be a blessing if you have young children and must look after them. After I found out that my dad had died, my toddler started crying for her lunch. She was hungry so I moved into autopilot and made her food. If you go swimming every Monday night, then gift yourself that routine and enjoy your exercise. If you volunteer or have a monthly girly night or weekly five-a-side football game, do these things. They all help to give structure to your life. Your loved one will be on their spirit journey towards healing: you can honour them by going on your healing journey.

Of course, if you need help then please ask for it. Many organisations are so helpful. I will list a few at the end of the book. Sometimes we need someone to listen who either is not family or is a professional with insights into our mind. Cruse Bereavement care in Scotland https://www.cruse.org.uk/get-help helped my younger daughter with the death of her granny, my mum-in-law. She could say whatever she wanted to the counsellor who listened and supported her. Communication is the key if you feel you are going under or cannot cope. Please reach out.

> *"Say not in grief that she is no more*
> *but say in thankfulness that she was*
> *A death is not the extinguishing of a light,*
> *but the putting out of the lamp*
> *because the dawn has come."*
> Rabindranath Tagore

I was writing the final draft of this book when I began lockdown for the COVID 19 pandemic. At the start of the self-isolation, there was a sense of something big coming and a fear of the unknown. It was only as time passed that I began to hear of COVID 19 deaths in Scotland. Bit by bit they became closer - a friend lost three family members over two weeks. My husband became intense in not allowing me to take mail or food deliveries into the house. Everything had to be sanitised by him. The initial lock-down was not too bad but in time I had a heavy sense of grief. I missed my daughters and my young grandson. The video call sessions were wonderful, but I missed the hugs and the way we all talked over one another when meeting in person. For every death I heard about in Scotland, there were hundreds in the USA where some of my dear friends lived. As I write there have been over thirteen million cases worldwide and over 500,000 deaths. Many could have been prevented if governments had reacted quicker and not put economies before lives.

Each day more deaths were announced on social media; adult children who lost their parents; whole nursing home populations being decimated; people who lost friends and neighbours; nursing and medical staff who died because they cared for us. At the start, I had decided to mark every post about death on Twitter with condolence to the family involved and a retweet with a hashtag #notjustastatistic. I had to give up with this after a few weeks because I simply could not keep up and was feeling sad and burdened every day. I was exhausted with other people's grief. My family was safe so far, but I felt raw and tearful on most days. I had not written about mass grief at all in this book. It simply had not occurred to me, even when I had written this grief chapter so many months previously. How could I have missed the effect that a tragedy with many deaths leaves imprinted on the communities involved?

My mum used to talk of the Aberfan tragedy in Wales where a primary school was buried under a landslide of slurry from the wastes of the local colliery. Many children were killed as well as adults. It stayed with her and she used to talk sadly about how she could not imagine the grief of the community left behind. I am sure that she empathised due to the death of her seven-year-old daughter many years previously. The day my mum was buried, the 13th March 1996, was marked by a huge tragedy in Scotland. We were on our way from the crematorium to the hotel for lunch when we were told that a man had entered a primary school in Dunblane and opened fire with a gun killing young children and a teacher. That, on top of my mum's passing, was almost unbearable. My mum had always said that she never understood how anyone could hurt an innocent child. I imagined her in the spirit world helping these children and sending succour to the parents left behind. The national grief was off the scale. The laws were changed to prevent ownership of an assault rifle. There were candlelit vigils and prayers and many tears. The town of Dunblane was never the same again. I do not believe Scotland was ever the same again. So, when I hear of yet another school killing in the USA and the lack of preventative legislation, I wonder how deep the wound is for those who live there? Thousands of children's voices have been silenced and thousands of parents, siblings, grandparents, aunts, and uncles have become the walking wounded. Life can become unbearable, especially if there is no change.

Then we have generational wounds and grief from genocide such as in Rwanda and the Holocaust. How do you grieve for millions of your own who have been murdered? How do you keep the memories alive? What does that degree of grief do to a population? I believe it leaves an indelible mark on those who follow. People build monuments and tell stories so that, in some way, the travesties can never be forgotten. Elie Wiesel, a Holocaust survivor says:

"I decided to devote my life to telling the story because I felt that having survived I owe something to the dead and anyone who does not remember betrays them again."

Black Elk talks of the effect that the genocide of Native Americans had on the People and their descendants:

"I did not know then how much was ended. When I look back now from this high hill of my old age, I can still see the butchered women and children lying heaped and scattered all along the crooked gulch as plain as when I saw them with eyes still young. And I can see that something else died there in the bloody mud and was buried in the blizzard. A people's dream died there. It was a beautiful dream..."

I believe that the grief that follows mass death either via natural tragedies like the Japanese tsunami, HIV and other pandemics, and the African or Irish famines or by evil intent like 9/11 or genocide, or by wars that lead to events like Hiroshima, maims huge communities and leaves a sense of destruction for eternities. These events can also leave a trail of guilt, shame, and revenge. The fissure in the connective earth energy creates disturbance felt around the world. We have no idea what effect that the rising of so many souls at one time can have on what is left behind. I am thankful for my belief in an afterlife when mass deaths happen. How else could we survive it? The thought of all these souls simply ceasing to exist at one moment in time would be too much to bear.

"Do not avert your eyes.
It is important
that you see this.
It is important that you feel
this."
Kamand Kojouri

Messages From The Spirit World

*"Perhaps they are not stars but rather
openings in Heaven where the love of our lost
ones shines down to let us know they are happy."*
Eskimo Legend

What follows are the stories kindly provided by my YouTube, Twitter, and Facebook followers with some of my own mixed in. They tell of their experiences after a spirit has passed either to them, through family or through mediums. I cannot thank all of you enough for sharing these heart-warming, beautiful stories and I am sure those reading this book feel the same way.

The following stories come from family or friends and show the beauty of messages if we are only open to them.

"My stepfather was diagnosed with terminal cancer about six years ago now. I was devastated. My whole family was, but me and Ernie were really close. My real dad died when I was six and Mam met Ernie about twelve years later and he was the father figure I had never known. Ernie was brought up Catholic but then didn't go to church. Mam never believed in anything, the same as my two brothers. I'm spiritual but I don't believe you need to go to church to talk to God. I just do it.

But Ernie 'got me.' He always said, "There's nothing wrong with you kidda. Nothing wrong with being different." He always called me 'kidda' even when I reached forty. Just before he passed away I was sitting by his bed and he turned to me and said,

"Do you think you live on after you die? Will I feel it? I am supposed to be Catholic but never went to church in my later life. Will that matter now?"

I turned to him with tears in my eyes and said, "Of course you live on. You are eternal. You are light and energy. Of course, you won't feel it going home. It's the most natural thing for your soul to do," I told him, "God doesn't care if you go to church. You believe in him, don't you? You're a good kind man and that's all that matters."

He reached across and held my hand and said, "I hope you're right kidda."

I smiled through my tears and said, "I promise and am so certain I want you to send me three signs the day you pass. That will make me realise that it's you and you're okay." He promised he would if he could. A few days later he passed away peacefully in his sleep.

I drove over to Mam's house as we had a lot of people to inform and planning to do. I still couldn't believe we had lost him, and my boys had lost the best grandad in the world. I took my two sons who were eleven and thirteen at the time. I sat at the kitchen table with Mam drinking tea and discussing funeral arrangements.

The boys were sitting on the sofa watching tv in the lounge next to us in the open-plan room when the tv suddenly went off. Mam couldn't understand what happened - no one had touched it.

She tried and tried to put it on; the power was there but no picture. So, we turned it off and left it. We would try again in an hour. About ten minutes later, on popped the tv that was turned off.

I laughed knowing it was Ernie...he knew how much Mam loved her tv and that would get her attention.

It got to lunchtime and we decided to get fish and chips. I took Jake my oldest son with me. The lady went out into the back of the shop. It was just me and Jake standing there not another soul which was unusual at lunchtime.

Then a piece of music came on the speakers. It was called, 'How long will l love you...as long as the stars are above you.' I froze as this song had only been out a few months and when l was alone driving or hearing it at home l used to pretend to sing it to Ernie because l loved him so much and the words were beautiful. I knew that was my second sign.

Once back at Mam's, Jake asked if he could borrow my phone for a minute. l said yes. He disappeared with it into the hall. Jake came running back in a minute later and said he took some photos and caught a ghost on Nana's stairs. He had taken several photos about a second apart. The last one showed a figure of a lady looking down smiling from the first landing. I zoomed in and saw it was the Virgin Mary. I showed Mam, who was so shocked she covered her mouth with her hand and said a swear word! I knew it was my last sign.

It was a sign from Ernie to say that 'Mother Mary from the Catholic church accepted me.' I was so happy he sent me the three signs. l have no doubt it was him. I knew all these signs that day were from Ernie telling me he was fine. I could almost hear him say

"You were right kidda it's all true."

"I still miss him terribly but I know I will see him again one day."

Lindsey

(PS: I asked Lindsey to send me the photo and indeed it does look like the Mother Mary - Colette)

"I had separated from my first husband and it would be the first Boxing Day that I wouldn't be with him and my daughters at my in-law's celebration. I had arranged to spend it at home with an old friend who was visiting his family for the festive season, but I was still sad. My husband's niece Helen was in spirit and I had always felt her about his family on Boxing Day. I was surprised when she appeared to me in my home, but she was frustrated because no one at my in-laws could sense her. She told me to phone her uncle, my ex, and let him know that she would be 'doing something with the Christmas tree lights'. I phoned and told him to watch what happened when I went off the phone. Helen nodded and disappeared. A few minutes later my ex phoned to say that the tree lights had gone out, then flashed slowly a few times, then gone out again before going back to normal. His niece Helen had made the lights dance, I am sure of it!"

Colette Clairvoyant

"I met my friend Jack back in 1979. I was fifteen, he was twenty-five. It was never a sexual thing (he was gay) and I found him annoying when we first met. He showed up at an important time in my life and our friendship was very nurturing for both of us but more so for me. He was like my uncle, aunt, father, mother, brother, and sister all rolled into one funny guy. He gave me unconditional love which I'd never had before.

So, Christmas that year (2013) was a Wednesday. I had planned to see him on the Monday evening. After work, I was just too tired. I was carrying a twelve pound turkey in my purse, so I cancelled. Fortunately, the Sunday prior I was out running last-minute errands and ran into him as we lived in the same area. That was huge because having cancelled on the Monday, had I not seen him on the Sunday I would have been tortured with guilt as he was dead by Wednesday morning. So, we went for coffee and blabbed. When we stopped to part ways he got teary-eyed and said, "You are my greatest accomplishment". He knew that so much of all the good I had found within was because of him. He wasn't bragging - he was just so proud of me and we both knew that his love was a pivotal factor in my becoming the person I am today (clean, sober, and spiritual). I would usually poo poo him or tell him to shut it when he said stuff like that, but I didn't this time. We hugged and said our 'I love yous' and made plans for the next weekend. So, Christmas morning I get up with the kids, do the stockings and go back to bed. My phone goes off and I ignore it, then it keeps going off, so I check and it's a text, one from a 'friend' who it was a bit odd to hear from. It read - call me asap. So, I call him, and he tells me that Jack is dead. I rush over to the building and cops and firemen won't let me near his apartment. The fire started in the kitchen. I think he was found on the floor and then whoever checked him put him on the bed. He suffered very few burns, it was the smoke, carbon monoxide that killed him (and his kitty named Stinky). Anyway, I'm devastated and shocked, the whole thing is just so unreal. Meanwhile, it's Christmas Day and I'm having people over for dinner so I'm in a fog robot daze. Turkey is cooking, I'm wandering around lost, Kim and her boyfriend are here and she's calling everyone to tell them. Then the smoke detector starts going nuts. There's no smoke, there's nothing. Then it goes off again, on and off for maybe five seconds at a time. I started to count because I felt it was Jack, it stopped and started at least twenty-two/twenty-three times. It's never done that before or since and like I said, it was not battery operated, it was electrical. I remember that I smiled. I mean I had nothing to smile about but this smile came out from within because I just knew it was Jack. Now the months after this are forgotten. I slept a lot, quit my job and I started to immerse myself in looking for meaning; answers about life and death, in understanding death, life and spirituality. I didn't dream of him for a long time, but other acquaintances/friends did, and I was so envious

I had so many weird experiences. I would sit in his car that was still parked behind his building and smoke cigarettes, cry and listen to sad songs. One time the sun was setting, and I thought - I don't know if I can do this. I don't know if I want to do this. How am I supposed to live without him in my life? And as I sat there contemplating ending my life, this huge tree branch crashed to the ground about fifteen feet from his car right in my line of vision where I was staring out. I said, "Alright alright, Jesus, Jack relax, I wasn't going to do it, God!"

Jack called me 'Luba' - just a silly name. The day we were driving to the unveiling of his tombstone, Kim, my friend, was driving, my son was in the back seat and my daughter was in Europe. So were going to pick up another of Jack's friends and were on this side street and this car starts slowly coming towards us but on the wrong side of the road. Kim and I are gesturing like 'What are you doing?' and the car stops in front of my side, and I look and can't help but notice the license plate-it says LUBA. I was like 'look, look!' My son texts my daughter to tell her (Jack and my kids were close) as she's just leaving an outdoor cafe somewhere in

Europe, she stops to read the text, looks up and the sign on the nail salon that she's stopped in front of is called 'Luba's'. How wild is that?"

Blessings, Tara

"I don't have a lot of memories of what I perceived as direct contact from my daughter who was named October, but I sometimes feel that she's directing me. My middle daughter has been encouraging (nagging) me to divest myself of some of the things of which I have far too many. I've been working hard at taking her advice. Last week when I was going through a box where I had put old bills and bank statements, I came across an envelope, addressed to me from Visiongift in Portland. It was a letter I had gotten on June 20th, 2014.

It started, "We at Lions Visiongift wish to thank the family members of October for her precious gift to the blind. Your decision to donate is deeply appreciated. We are very pleased to inform you that this donation did result in two corneal transplants and two individuals who were blind have an opportunity to regain their sight. This gift represents a living Memorial to your daughter - a memorial to a person who believed enough in life to share its beauties."

Carolyn

"My mum's friend was Mrs. Webster. She lived across the landing from us in the building I lived in from age sixteen to twenty-one. She had also lived across the landing from my wee gran Isobel for many years along the road. So I knew her as both my gran's friend and also my mum's. She became very precious to me after my own gran passed. Her husband was called Peter and he had lost his legs due to vein problems caused by smoking. In the run-up to my first wedding, Peter was preparing a present for us. He had a hobby of painting and was very good in an old-fashioned way. If I popped into the house there was mayhem as a painting was covered up. Our wedding present was amazing. It was a painting of a mountain in the Lake District of England and had pride of place in our first home. Peter was a man of few words, but he expressed himself beautifully through his artwork. My honeymoon had been in Venice, a city that I love even more than Glasgow! I have visited it a few times in my life and never tire of the light and beauty of it all. We went to Venice again not long after Peter died. It was there that I had a glimpse of what Spirit life might be like.

We had arrived off the waterbus in front of the Doges Palace and I was walking towards the two obelisks that face into the lagoon. The crowds were milling about, the gondoliers were whistling, and the heat rose from the ground. I caught my breath and stopped dead. In front of one of the obelisks was Peter! He raised his hand and waved at me. He had an easel in front of him and appeared to be painting the Doges Palace by the way he was facing. He looked very tanned and happy and he had both his legs! He was staring at me and I could see a small smile. Then he raised his hand as though to wave. My husband looked at me as though 'what now?' and I told him. When I looked back Peter was gone. I knew I had seen his spirit but was baffled as to why I had seen it in Venice. I was happy for him though. What a stunning place to visit as a spirit.

When I next visited Gran Webster at her flat, I knew I would have to tell her but had no idea how she would take it. She smiled and had a wee cry. She told me that before Peter had joined the civil service as his main job, he had studied art in Venice, and it was a place he loved with all his heart. This made me happy about my belief in the afterlife. Isn't it lovely to know that something or somewhere that was precious to you in life can still be available to you in death? It is like your own personalised heaven!"

Colette Clairvoyant

"Ed was a musician. He has manipulated the CD player when I listened to one of his CDs. He made the CD install without me pressing the remote. After listening to his singing, I ejected the CD, put the remote down, and got up to retrieve the CD. The CD went back into the machine and the first song 'I Love You for Sentimental Reasons' played. He did that on several different occasions, almost taking off a finger once.

I wanted to let Eddie's friends know how he was communicating with me. It was a great comfort to me. I thought it would be a comfort to them but some of his friends were ex-girlfriends and Eddie and I were not together when he died. I wasn't sure that everyone would understand the psychic connection. I didn't want anyone to feel hurt. I thought I would write a message on a Christmas card. At the store, I saw a funny card with Star Trek/Santa humour that Ed would have bought in life. But I didn't know if Eddie would like me to use a more spiritual card. I decided to place my hand above the box of three different cards, in turn, to see if I would "feel" a difference. I put my hand above the first box of cards, a very religious picture, and sentiment. I didn't feel anything. The same with the second box with a generic season's greeting. By now I'm only feeling a little silly. When I placed my hand above the box of humorous cards, the box flew at me, hitting me in the chest and then falling to the floor.

The following Christmas season, I was singing 'All I Want for Christmas is You' while I unpacked Christmas decorations in the loft when a paperback book flew off the shelf.

Once I thought I saw him walk behind the choir at a Christmas vigil mass. A year later another friend of mine who sees dead people, told me that she and her daughter saw the same person I saw walk past but who seemingly disappeared."

Patricia (Pat)

"My stepdad Martin was diagnosed with a malignant brain tumour in 2000. I was 18 at the time. It was caught late. There was the option to try to remove the tumour which was high risk, or he was going to die. The operation was agreed due to the fact he had zero chance of survival otherwise. An artery was cut in his brain that paralysed him. They said a stroke, but he couldn't move or talk for the remainder of his life.

We brought him home and our front room became a hospital room fully equipped with bed and hospital machinery. My Mum quit her job, became bound to the flat, and nursed him until his passing.

He was a wonderful man, very patient, intelligent, funny, and loving. This was unjust, to say the least. I'd never seen him angry or frustrated. He was a very calm person. The torment in his eyes, the only expression of how he felt, was apparent the whole time. We never got to hear how he felt about it all. Several months later he passed in the middle of the night.

Several years gone, same apartment. My Mum was in a relationship with someone called Cliff and the front room had become the bedroom. I actually can't remember why her bed was in the front room. I think we were re-carpeting or decorating upstairs at the time.

As they laid together, he told my Mum he loved her. With no windows open in the house, no breeze, the door right next to them swung back and slammed shut.

This was a very blatant paranormal occurrence. I included all of the above because I now realise the bed they were laying in was in the same spot my stepdad's bed was where he had passed away."

Crystal

"In the midst of all this, my dad visited me in a dream. It was such an amazing lucid dream. I will remember it always. My dad often communicates through dreams. In the dream, we were looking out at the view of North Berwick, a place where we used to have holidays. I remember saying that it would be perfect if Mum were here and he indicated she was and pointed to the cafe on top of a hill where she was sitting reading, her favourite thing in the world. I was happy that she was with us, but dad urged me to look at the sea view. He pointed to the two bays split by the harbour which had lots of little boats bobbing up and down peacefully. Then he pointed out to sea and I could see a large wave like a tsunami coming towards the shore. It was travelling fast. It hit the first bay and wrecked all the little boats and I remember feeling so sad and also worried that the other bay, that had a children's' paddling pool in it, would be decimated too. But he showed me that the harbour wall and the rocks had absorbed the wave and the second bay was still calm and safe. Then he nodded as though to say 'understand' which I didn't. Then I woke up.

I was worried because I know that water in a dream means emotions and here my dad had shown me a big wave of emotion coming towards the shore that had wrecked everything in its path. Yet he had also shown me that one bay was still safe and calm and untouched. I resolved to wait and see but prepared myself for this emotional tsunami by getting ahead with work. It hit two days later when an incident happened to my nephew that was so intensely unfair that it made the news and eventually the law was changed because of it. I was so worried but felt that he would find a safe harbour where it was calm, as my dad had suggested in the dream. Yet I felt there was a lesson still to hit as I couldn't pinpoint what the wrecked boats meant. The next day I opened the newspaper only to see that a large wave had hit the bays of North Berwick and wrecked all the boats in the harbour! My dad had not just shown me a metaphysical meaning in the dream but had directly shown me what was going to happen to his beloved harbour. And to think he used to hate all this 'spooky' stuff.

Colette Clairvoyant

"My dad passed away in 1996. He had been sick and in and out of the hospital for two years. When he passed, I asked for a sign that he was okay. I hadn't had someone close to me pass away since my grandmother passed when I was seven years old. When we were at the cemetery, waiting for the priest to arrive, I glance over at the trip odometer and it read "313". I thought that was so weird because 3/13 is my birthday. A week or so later, my family was together, and I told them about the odometer showing 313. My sister then told me that the family flowers for the wake were $313. The dinner after the funeral was $313 and my brother's co-workers collected $313 for our family. I felt like that was the sign I needed that he was okay. I felt much better."

Gina

"My father always called me "Kit" (short for kitten) until he passed away on June 14, 2005. In December 2005, I was standing in a long Barnes and Noble (bookstore) line waiting to purchase books for Christmas Gifts. I was looking at a little Barnes and Noble shelf/stand that was set up next to where I was in line. I glanced over and saw a cute little Christmas card. On the front of the card was a baby kitten, wearing a red Santa Hat. When I opened the card, the written message read, "Merry Christmas Kitten". This card was out of place (no other Christmas cards were where this card was). It was like someone got the card, changed their mind, and set the card on this little stand. Maybe it is my mind, but in my heart, I believe it was my dad's way of wishing me a Merry Christmas.

In my house, I have an office. In this office, I have my dad's army medals hanging on a wall. My fiancé's son, Chris, is autistic and deaf. I looked up one day and saw Chris was in the office (I keep the door closed). But Chris was in this room, and I watched him. I saw him render a military salute. But I could only physically see that Chris was the only one in the room. Chris has never met my dad. So, I find it interesting to see Chris render a military salute. One thing my dad used to tell me, 'truth is stranger than fiction'."

Jackie J.A

"After a move to a new place, I decided to buy something that would remind me of Jim and at a store that sells pillows, I saw one beige and brown with a stuffed dog on it, so I bought it and chose a special place to display it. A few months passed. I was sad going through eye worries with possible glaucoma diagnosis and was afraid of losing my sight. Suddenly, the eyes on the dog on the pillow came to life. I checked the whole room for reflections, for lights, for TV flashes, wondering what caused the flashing eyes and all of a sudden complete peace of mind regarding my vision engulfed my whole body and soul. I knew I would be alright, and I heard Jim's voice say that his worst worry was losing his hearing...and mine was my sight! He managed quite well with his hearing assist companion, his service dog Captain Daisy. She was his guide while Jim kayaked on his Cardi-Yak Expedition and while Jim drove his car alerting him to sirens and noises on the road. I felt Jim's presence right by my side as he had promised before he passed away to the Afterlife."

Colette from Canada

"As for signs, I had one that comes regularly when my grandfather or dad or grandmother comes to visit me. It is a smell of something that I can remember being associated with them individually. Like the fragrance of old spice that my grandfather would splash on his face after shaving. My dad, it would be a song from Monty Python's Life of Brian movie. My grandmother, it is a smell of smoke, as she was a heavy smoker, and floral scent."

Ann Brown

"My friend Dan recently passed. He loved music. He used to post a lot of songs on Facebook. He has a lot of pages and groups that post songs. One day I went on and the first things that came up on my newsfeed was a page that posted two songs in a row: "Daniel" (his name) by Elton John and "I Feel Free" a song by Cream (his favourite band)! I took a picture with my phone so I could show a friend. When I looked at the picture again it showed "Dan". Then I saw the vertical word "music". Dan, as I told you, loved his music. I took a picture of it. Today, I looked at the picture and saw in the upper left-hand corner, the word "beer". Beer was his favourite drink. Another time I saw his name again, "Dan". Then the word "satellite" formed. He lived near Satellite Beach! I also noticed one song had four "likes, the other had twenty-one "likes". His birthday was 4/21."

Gina

"Yesterday is a memory, tomorrow is
a mystery and today is a gift,
which is why it is called the present.
What the caterpillar perceives is the end;
to the butterfly is just the beginning.
Everything that has a beginning has an ending.
Make your peace with that and all will be well."
Buddhist Saying

Messages From Mediums who passed on proof of the afterlife.

"One night I was reading for a lovely woman when her mum came through from Spirit. The woman had been crying as she missed her mum so much. It had been nearly five years, but she had not stopped grieving even a little. Her mum asked me to pass on that she wanted her to stop crying all the time. This seemed to make my client worse. She cried even more. The spirit then said, "Ask her to try to stop crying and I will show her I am around her." I passed this on, and the woman dried her eyes and said that if her mum wanted that she would try. At that very moment, a glass candle holder that I had loved for years exploded into lots of shards of glass and the candle went out! My client and I were so shocked that all we could do was stare at it and then at one another. The spirit had done what she said she would do - she had shown without doubt that when her daughter stopped crying, she had made her presence felt. We both ended up laughing and reminiscing about our bossy mums."

Colette Clairvoyant

"I wanted to share this story with you. It was what made me 'believe'.

For a long time, I had vivid dreams, things moved at home, feathers turned up, my mother woke me from sleep to inform me of my husband's infidelity. Yet I still tried to find a rational explanation.

Mum was Jehovah's Witness and they believe fortune tellers are very bad and when you are gone you are gone. Anyway, after a long internal battle, I booked up to see a lovely lady who is a medium and now years on, my friend. As soon as I went through the door I felt calm and happy. We sat out in her garden with a cuppa.

Mum came through immediately. Pam described her and Mum told her things - silly things that only she and I knew including a game my daughter and I played of 'hairdressers'. She even got the name 'Ethyl Methyl' who was a naughty angry customer I used to pretend to be. So much validation!

Then she said, "Did you like the butterflies?" I said I love butterflies. She said, "No your mum is saying she has sent you butterflies." I said not that I can think of.

Well as I drove into my drive, a butterfly flew around my car several times and right up through my windscreen dead centre. Okay, I thought, very clever, thanks Mum.

The next day was my birthday. I went out to my front garden and I have never seen so many butterflies in my life. At least a hundred, maybe more. Over every single bush. It was the most beautiful gift. I closed my eyes and thanked Mum. From that moment on my spiritual journey began."

Kathy

"I visited a medium for the first time and she asked if I itched in my hair a lot. I told her I have a tick where I always itch on the top of my head ever since I was young. She said that's your mum letting you know she's nearby. Our mum died when I was ten and my sister was nine. Afterward, I rang my sister and she had just gone through a very messy break up with her partner, and she told me throughout this difficult time her head had itched so badly she had gone to see the doctor afraid she had head lice.

I was also told my mum sends me butterflies by the same medium. This rang true to me because I moved to Australia with my Australian husband and we were living in a basic shack whilst we built the house we live in now. Often I was homesick for the UK and my family and most mornings I would see hordes of butterflies flying in formation. I saw this so often I mentioned to my husband, telling him that Australia was full of butterflies! My sister and I got joint tattoos of butterflies in memory of our mum."

Russ

"We started holding weekly development circles and weekly mediumship nights. On one such night, I had such a lovely message from my mum from a medium I respected very much. His name was Max and he had such a lovely nature and kindness just shone from him. He knew that I was very sceptical and had a science background and felt that mediumship should in some way offer proof of the afterlife and be specific. Max was one of the best and I always felt his messages were clear and directed at the correct people. By that, I mean that he could pinpoint who he wished to talk to rather than say, 'I have a message for someone near the back, etc'. My mum was called Mary and I was always a bit doubtful when someone gave me her name because it is such a popular name in her age group. So, Max approached me before the mediumship evening. I had clients in my room that night so wouldn't be part of the event. He said he had a message from my mum. He said that she wasn't giving her name because 'that wouldn't convince me'. I laughed at that because that was very true. Then Max said something I will remember forever. He said,

"Your mum says that her *three* knees are fine." This meant so much to me because it was a joke between me and my mum. She had a knee replacement on her left knee and then a few years later another on her right knee. Before she died she had the left knee replaced again. We always said that she had three knees. Now *that* message was proof it was my mum. Max was one of the best mediums I have ever met."

Colette Clairvoyant

"My oldest sister died a little over a year ago. Since that time, she has shown me many signs that her spirit is still roaming the universe. The best sign yet would have to be the time she interrupted my phone call. One night, I couldn't sleep because I was missing her, so I just spoke out loud and told her that I loved her. The next morning, my fiancé's mother asked me to call her. She messaged me her number since I didn't have it already, and I keyed it in. We had been talking on the phone for a while when all of a sudden I heard complete silence on the other end. I pulled the phone away from my ear and a little box popped up at the bottom of the screen that said the call had been lost. I looked up and noticed that the numbers typed in on the keypad was a sequence of three numbers that happened to be in the middle of my sister's phone number, which was still saved in the contacts of my phone. She let me know that she had heard me loud and clear."

Tiasha B

"My mum had been ill and was taken to the hospital just before Christmas 2014. She was diagnosed with leukaemia and was started on treatment right away. I was not allowed to visit her because I had a bad cold and she was immunosuppressed. I was so worried about her and missed her so much. Sadly, she had a heart attack and died between Christmas and New Year. I was devastated as were all her children and her grandchildren.

A few months later, my soul sister Colette messaged me to tell me about the dream she had that felt very important. My mum had shown herself in the dream and Colette knew who she was right away. My mum showed herself standing at a table and Colette said that she had five envelopes before her. She also had five silver charms in her hand and was very precise at placing one charm in each envelope while indicating to Colette that this was the important bit.

My mum gave her granddaughters a silver charm every Christmas to add to their charm bracelets. There were five granddaughters and five charms and envelopes. My mum had been hospitalised before she had time to wrap these for her granddaughters. She died but the charms were in her house. I knew my mum was telling me to make sure that her beloved granddaughters received their gifts from her one last time. This made me sad but also happy that my mum was doing fine and was still thinking of her family even as she went on her own healing journey."

Sooz, Aberdeenshire

How To Prepare for a Good Death

"When your time comes to die, be not like those whose hearts are filled with fear of death, so that when their time comes they weep and pray for a little more time to live their lives over again in a different way. Sing your death song and die like a hero going home."
Tecumseh

When couples embark on the process of having a baby, they may muse and prepare in equal measure. They muse about the baby's gender, the names they like, when it may happen, and so on. They prepare by looking at finances, childcare potentials, becoming healthy, and taking preconception multivitamins. After conception takes place, they prepare even more for the birth itself. They look at options for birthing, midwives, doulas, whether they want a home birth or hospital birth. They seek advice on diet, minor ailments, and what tests they should have for the baby. As the birth draws nearer in time, they ask for help with other children and sort out who will be at the birth. They plan, plan, and plan some more. Even the best-laid plans can come unstuck, but at least there is a potential plan that can alert health carers and family as to the needs and wishes of the pregnant woman.

Conception and birth are at the start of the soul's voyage on earth. Death is the birth of our new spiritual voyage to the afterlife. Yet how much do we plan for a good death? What plans, if any, are offered to our loved ones, and who may be with us as we end this life and have massive roles to play as to our care, our wishes, or our simple spiritual needs? Putting it so bluntly, we can see how horrific our western culture is in preparing for the rebirth of our souls. The birth of a baby is a happy and upbeat time whereas the crossing over of a loved one is sad and devastating for those left behind. But the taboo around actually accepting that a loved one will die is simply holding back conversations that not only would help the person who will pass but also the potential grief process of those left behind.

We do not know when death will come. It could be a long-drawn-out process where the necessity to talk and plan could be tackled. It could be sudden and totally unexpected. In all circumstances, isn't it just wise to have some sort of personal plan that is known, to a loved one? In my career as a medium, so many people asked me if I could tell them if their mum or dad who passed was happy with how they handled the funeral or the gifting of special mementos. It is not morbid to think about things deeper and leave more than a drawer with insurance policies.

One of the best gifts you could ever gift yourself is to prepare for your passing. One of the best gifts that you could give your loved ones, is to prepare them for your passing. When you prepare for your death and share your preparations with even just one trusted family member, then you are taking away a burden in advance. I am not just talking about the practical issues - as you prepare yourself spiritually, emotionally, and mentally, you are showing a concern that loved ones will know that you have had a good life and are contented enough to plan for your passing. What a gift for your family! Imagine, leaving behind loved ones who know that you were in no fear, that you were spiritually prepared and emotionally and mentally present while making plans. Once you have made your plans and are happy and contented that all is well and covered, you can get on with living life to the full. To know that you said what you needed or wanted to say, that people knew how precious they were to you and that they also knew what your requests for your funeral are, is simply life-affirming and to me, actually easier than saying nothing at all and hoping people can guess or know your feelings, needs and wants.

Let us look at some areas we can try to prepare ahead in so that we can get on with living and our loved ones can see and sense that we understand and accept our mortality. If we can set the stage as such, for a future production, then we can forget about it and simply live. This is always a work in progress and can be done gently and with compassion - no need to freak them out!

Preparing Spiritually

If you have a religion or path that has guidance on how to prepare for the afterlife, then read up on it or take wisdom from an elder or priest/priestess. Talk to your family about any particular death rituals that are precious to you and who should perform any rites at services. Write it down.

Live the life that your beliefs encapsulate. Walk your talk with a gentle energy that shows that you are truly living.

Honour your path but do not proselytise or force anyone to take part in a service or ritual in which they may feel uncomfortable.

If you have spiritual objects that mean a lot to you, write down what you want to happen to them. This can be incredibly special as you can plan who could be gifted what and know that your beloved items will go to who may need them or treasure them.

Face any spiritual fears you may have and work with them. If you have doubts, address them. Show your loved ones an inner strength that will convince them that you are not afraid of moving from one spiritual realm to another. To be content spiritually in life is also to be content spiritually as we approached death.

Preparing Emotionally

In my experience, most people fear not being around their loved ones and losing connection rather than death itself. To prepare yourselves emotionally it would be easy to think that we should detach from the people that we love to make it easier when our time comes, but to live a detached life without vulnerability is simply no way to live. Love makes us vulnerable.

People also fear the dying experience with potential pain rather than death itself. It is alright to be fearful of pain, loss, and how your loved ones will cope after you have passed. This is natural and can only be addressed by realising that the human spirit is amazing, and humans can cope and adjust to almost anything. We all lose our loved ones, we all die. We cannot believe we will cope but somewhere deep inside we know we will – because we must. Life does go on. If we can accept that our daughters and sons will go on to recover and have good lives, then we can enjoy growing older and watching them develop and help them be strong enough to thrive rather than survive.

If the people we would leave behind may be incapacitated such as a disabled child or a dependent spouse, then we need to make plans for their care so that we can avoid anxiety for both them and us.

Look at how you feel when you are worried about your passing. Name the emotions and aim to understand the reasons why and address them. This may be an ongoing exercise.

Preparing Mentally

If we have mental health issues that focus on death in a debilitating way, then we should strive to have counselling and therapy to address them. I believe that a fear of death could manifest more intensely if we have an underlying mental health issue such as depression or anxiety. It would be important to get help with any mental health issue first.

Preparing Physically

This may seem a bit of a misnomer - to prepare physically for a good death when your physicality is what will be left behind. Yet by understanding your physical health issues and potential decline, optimising your medication regime to prevent excessive pain or debilitation, you will be able to be in stable health for longer and have more control.

Some people choose to hide their infirmities from loved ones but then, when there is a decline, it can seem so marked as to be unbearable. In my opinion, it is better to include loved ones in care and decisions regarding health. This way they remain in the loop and trust that you are sharing the truth with them.

There can be such intimacy in allowing a partner to, for example, help you shower or a grown-up child to help tend to your physical needs. This takes trust and it is up to you to find that trust and if it is not there then to work on building it.

Preparing Practically

There are obvious things that can be addressed practically from writing a will to having a savings policy so that your loved ones are in no financial hardship when your time comes to pass. Planning the practical aspects can be easier than planning emotionally and can also be a gift to yourself as well as those who will be left behind.

If you can plan in your head what you would wish for your funeral, and then pass it on or write it down, then you will absolve them from any guilt they may feel for maybe getting it wrong. This can also be done as a family group and be made funny and upbeat even though there will be a deeper serious side to it.

The celebration of your life would include things that are precious to you and that can be certain songs, smells, prayers, or hymns. You may not want people to mourn in black. You may want to be 'planted' under a tree. Your passing, funeral, and memorial should reflect you as a person so let there be no doubt who that person is! I have a friend who is a lifelong Duran Duran fan. I fully expect there to be singing along to them at her funeral some way down the line, because, well, it would not be her day if we did not.

Once you have prepared financially and have expressed your wishes for your send-off, you can get back to the day to day beauty of living life. You can investigate things like Swedish Death Cleaning or Kon Mari method to declutter your home and possessions because no one should leave a lifetime's hoarding for loved ones to sort out. By decluttering you will also begin to feel lighter and less trapped by things. Keep things that are important but get rid of any excess tat that no one will want and would be an embarrassment to be remembered by, anyway!

Whether your death is sudden or a long goodbye, if you are prepared and have prepared your loved ones, then you will have a good death.

Acknowledgments

I had major synergy this morning. I had a friend who died recently, and I was thinking about her and what we talked about last night with her grieving husband. At her funeral and after, everyone just talked about how kind she was and how she cared deeply about people and her animals. It made me think - what a wonderful way to end this book! Simply to finish with the legacy of kindness. I was mulling it over and thinking should I put her name 'Lorraine' in it. I felt she might like that but wasn't 100% sure. Then my phone buzzed, and it was a message from 'Lorraine'...not my friend who passed but another lady asking for healing for her husband. I hadn't heard from that 'Lorraine' for three years. So, I am taking the synergy of the name as a sign that my friend Lorraine wants her name in this book. This makes me happy. Thank you for your kindness and support, Lorraine. I hope to be remembered as being kind too.

The writing of this book has been both difficult and uplifting. I have cried many tears while reading the stories and messages that people gave me. Crafting a book with so many voices has been difficult. I hope that it helps those who need it.

I would like to thank my daughter Jennifer and her husband Craig for giving me the best gift ever - my first grandchild, Alexander. I have dedicated this book to him because he is after all, what it is about - life! From being the infant who struggled to be safely born to the big one-year-old he is now; he has given Jim and I a new lease of life.

Big thanks are due to my daughter Jillian for her staunch support for this book. It was a hard book to write at times, but she encouraged me to see the destination and to work towards it. To Peter, for encouragement and for laughing at my silly memes.

I would also like to thank my beta readers- Jim, Sooz, Jennifer, Jillian, and Wendy. Your advice and support kept me writing. Of course, big thank you to Andrea for helping with the editing.

To Jim, my wonderful husband, who is my cheerleader extraordinaire - I thank you for putting up with my anxiety about making this the best I could manage, especially during COVID 19 lock-down when I was missing my girls and was emotional.

Thank you to all the spirits who have connected to me in my personal life and my readings. You have given me the glimpses of the afterlife to allow me to write with some clarity. Blessings and thanks to my guide, White Storm, who, as ever, is never far away when I need him. All praise to Goddess Saraswati whose guidance and creativity flowed to me when I asked.

Thank you to all the people who contributed their wonderful stories about death, dying, bereavement, and the afterlife. I cannot thank you all enough. It has been very hard to edit down your words as they have all been inspiring and very personal. I hope I have done this with care and attention and have not lost the intensity and love in your stories. I would also like to thank those who sent me their stories that for one reason or another, didn't make it into the book. I read every single one of them and am sorry I couldn't put them all in this book.

So, thank you to Agnieszka, Sylvie, Colette from Canada, Shona, Britney, Angela, Eugene, Stephanie, Rachel, Ruby, Hanne Jahr, T.J, Kathleen, Kathy, Juanita, Ragnhild, Joyce, Tina, Kristi,

Nicoletta, Nancy, Jo, Ruth, Kristen, E.H, Carolyn, Laurie, Carrie Woomer, Lindsey, Tara, Ann, Patricia, Kathy, Crystal, Russ, Gina, Tiasha, Jackie and Sooz. Also, to all who wanted to be anonymous. Many blessings to you all!

References

All chapter quotes unless from books, friends, or in the public domain are from the websites below.

https://mostphrases.blogspot.com/

https://www.wiseoldsayings.com/suicidal-thoughts-quotes/#ixzz6M9C8e9pk

https://www.loveliveson.com/loss-of-pet-quotes/

https://www.giftsforyounow.com/blog/pet-memorial-quotes/

https://www.wiseoldsayings.com

https://lifeafterdeath.com/

Goodreads 'Promise Me, Dad' by Joe Biden MacMillan

Resources

Here are some links for advice and help

https://www.samaritans.org

https://www.mind.org.uk

https://www.mariecurie.org.uk help with a terminal illness

https://www.mariecurie.org.uk for cancer care

https://www.cruse.org.uk bereavement care

https://www.lullabytrust.org.uk/ support for sudden infant death

https://www.alzheimers.org.uk/

USA

http://www.hospicefoundation.org/

Thank you so much for reading this far. Many blessings. Please have a look at my YouTube spiritual channel 'Colette Clairvoyant' for videos on spirituality and mediumship.

https://www.youtube.com/channel/UCBMUDdSXne0U25P-I4OuoHA

You can contact me on

stormwarrior41@aol.com

My Amazon book page is

https://www.amazon.co.uk/Colette-Brown/e/B005HYG49K/ref=dp_byline_cont_pop_book_1

"No one wants to die. Even people who want to go to heaven don't want to die to get there. And yet death is the destination we all share. No one has ever escaped it. And that is as it should be because Death is very likely the single best invention of Life. It is Life's change agent. It clears out the old to make way for the new."
Steve Jobs

Printed in Great Britain
by Amazon